J RICHARDSON
684248 .

THE
LITTLE
HISTORY
OF
OXFORDSHIRE

THE

LITTLE
HISTORY

OF

OXFORDSHIRE

PAUL SULLIVAN

For Magda, Jan and Theo;
remembering our momentous years in Oxfordshire.

First published 2019

The History Press
The Mill, Brimscombe Port
Stroud, Gloucestershire, GL5 2QG
www.thehistorypress.co.uk

British Library Cataloguing in Publication Data.
A catalogue record for this book is available from the British Library.

ISBN 978 0 7509 8802 5

Typesetting and origination by The History Press
Printed in Turkey

CONTENTS

INTRODUCTION

In acceding to the request to compile a summary of the historical material on which the Early History of Oxford was based, I did not at the moment quite realise what I had undertaken.

James Parker, 1885

The apology quoted above was written in the preface to the new edition of James Parker's *Early History of Oxford, 727–1100*. He had underestimated the time it would take to dig through the historical material, and was late getting his book to the publisher. Armed as I am with the Internet's bottomless pit and a huge database based on research from my previous Oxfordshire books, I have fewer excuses than Parker. But I know exactly how he felt.

In terms of its importance in the political, artistic, scientific and social history of Britain, Oxfordshire is equalled only by London. A lot of this is due to the magnetic pull of the university, which has tasted unfair riches of celebrity residents over the centuries. The history of Oxford is in many ways the history of England.

This is what makes it so challenging when considering the county as a whole – trying to balance the ogre of Oxford against the rest of Oxfordshire. So, my approach here has been to fight off Oxford as much as possible, knowing full well that the ogre will loom large without my help. The stories included here were chosen primarily for their entertainment value, punctuated with summaries of the background social and political upheavals that defined each era, to give the flow of history a coherence which, in reality, it most certainly never had.

Oxfordshire presents several faces to the world. It encompasses the Cotswolds, the Chilterns, the North Wessex Downs, 'Banburyshire' in the north, Oxford in the south, and a large section, centred on Abingdon, wrested from Berkshire in 1974. A large chunk of it was formerly a royal hunting forest, plonked like a decadent Eden between the rivers Evenlode and Windrush, smothering the land from Burford in Oxfordshire to Bernewood in Buckinghamshire. Most of it was lopped during the seventeenth-century Civil Wars, and the Enclosure Acts mopped up what was left – examples of the many and surprising ways in which history moulds the physical and moral landscape we take for granted.

A brief word about anachronism. I have used the name 'Oxfordshire' throughout, even when talking about pre-Anglo-Saxon history. The county didn't exist before the tenth century AD, but I have grudgingly followed convention and applied the tag to the early bits too. The assertion that Romans, Catuvellauni, and even dinosaurs, gambolled through the thoroughfares of Oxfordshire is nonsense; but there are only so many times you can say things like 'the part of the country currently known as Oxfordshire' without losing patience, sanity and readers, in that order.

The timelessness of Oxford and Oxfordshire is just an illusion. They sometimes pretend to be academic and bucolic relics of a Golden Age, but in reality, the city and county have always been at the forefront of progress. For every thatched Cotswold stone cottage there is an office expanding the digital possibilities of modern life; for every former mill there is a Bicester Village designer brand outlet; and for every traditional Morris team there is The Next Big Thing playing in a pub near you (probably The Jericho Arms in Oxford).

All of which makes me think – why on earth would I ever want to live anywhere else?

Paul Sullivan, 2019

IN THE BEGINNING WAS ...?

A history of Oxfordshire has to start somewhere. The historian in me says it should kick off with the earliest recorded mention of Oxford, in an Anglo-Saxon Chronicle entry from the year 912; or perhaps with the earliest human settlers more than a thousand years earlier.

However, the imaginary Richard Dawkins perched on my right shoulder disagrees. He says it should all start with the first mammals, or the dinosaurs. But then Stephen Hawking on my left shoulder insists that it should go back much further and begin with Big Bangs and meteorites. The *Launton meteorite*, specifically.

This lump of interstellar rock, born in our embryonic solar system at some point between the Big Bang and the formation of the earth, crashed to the ground in a garden at Launton, near Bicester, at 7.30 p.m. on 15 February 1830. According to a report in the *Magazine of Natural History* of 1831:

> Its descent was accompanied with a most brilliant light, which was visible for many miles around, and attended with a triple explosion … A man named Thomas Marriot was passing near the garden at

the moment, and states that it came rapidly towards him from the
north-east, not perpendicularly but obliquely, appearing about the
size of a cricket-ball; and that expecting it would strike him, he
instinctively lowered his head to avoid it.

So, having satisfied the Hawking in me, I must now
appease my inner Dawkins and make honourable mention of the region's early habitats and wildlife.

Oxfordshire is rich in fossils, and was an important
source of material for early scientists trying to deter-
mine the true nature of petrified shells and bones. In the
north-west of the county Jurassic limestone, shale and
sandstone forms the Cotswold hills, the origin of the
famously golden-yellow Cotswold Stone that decorates
many a town and village in these parts. Locally tagged
seams include Banbury Marble, Stonesfield Slate and
Forest Marble (named after Wychwood Forest), which
has yielded a rich fossil harvest.

These relics caused headaches for seventeenth-century
Robert Plot, first keeper of the Ashmolean Museum in
Oxford. Fossilised seashells found inland posed the obvious question: how did they come to be here in the rocks
of Oxfordshire, so far from the sea?

Plot refused to believe that England could experience
earthquakes sufficient to raise cockle beds to hill-top
level. He also ruled out another popular theory of the
time – that the Biblical Deluge, of Noah's Ark fame, was
responsible. If the Flood had been a gentle accumulation
of water, Plot reasoned, it would not have evicted the
shellfish from their sea beds and left them stranded on hills
and mountains; and, if violent, it would have scattered the
animals rather than leaving them in the neat, ordered beds
he had observed. Crowded shellfish beds suggested that

these were established colonies that would have needed far longer than the Flood's forty days to become rooted.

Robert Plot had a couple of alternative theories. He suggested that urinous salts – i.e. fossilised puddles of urine – may have been involved in some deposits. But his chief theory was that fossils were formed at the beginning of Creation, when God was 'dispersing the Seminal Virtue of Animals through the Universe'. When this divine outpouring hit water, it resulted in living shellfish; but if the creative juices hit 'an improper Matrix' such as earth, they produced shellfish-shaped inanimate stones.

OF DINOSAURS AND OTHER GIANTS

The grand matriarch of Oxfordshire wildlife is the Megalosaurus, a carnivore from the Middle Jurassic. Robert Plot, the man with the fossil theories mentioned above, had the first crack at identification. He examined a thigh bone, discovered at Cornwell near Oxford, and went against received opinion by rejecting the theory that it belonged to a Roman-era elephant. He suggested instead that it was evidence of an ancient race of humanoid giants.

The truth, finally nailed in the early 1800s, would have been as outrageous to Robert Plot as his giants theory seems to us. The bone belonged to a previously unsuspected group of enormous reptiles. When Oxford University canon William Buckland discovered further remains of the creature at Stonesfield, he named the animal *Megalosaurus bucklandii*. In 1842, Richard Owen, professor of the Royal College of Surgeons in London, placed Megalosaurus in a new class of animals – the dinosaurs.

Megalosaurus at Woodstock Museum.
(Photo by Magdalena Sullivan)

Oxfordshire proved to be a hotspot for dinosaur finds. Remnants of all the following beasts can be viewed in the Oxford University Museum of Natural History (OUMNH). *Cetiosaurus oxoniensis*, translating as 'Oxford whale lizard', was a Brontosaurus-type beast, unearthed at Chipping Norton in 1825, and another at Kirtlington in 1860. *Eustreptospondylus oxoniensis* ('Oxford well-turned vertebra'), belonged to the family that later produced the Tyrannosaurus rex. It was discovered in 1871 in a brick pit at Summertown in Oxford. *Camptosaurus prestwichii*, a member of the iguanodon family, came to light at a brick pit on Cumnor Hurst, south-west of Oxford, in 1880.

Ardley is the only place in Britain to have been given the status of Site of Special Scientific Interest (SSSI) on account of its dinosaur footprints. The 165-million-year-old tracks, embedded in the Jurassic limestone, were made by a Megalosaurus and a herd of Cetiosaurs. They were discovered in 1997, and the SSSI designation came in 2010, the Megalosaurus tracks having been carefully removed and reinstalled at the Oxfordshire Museum in Woodstock in 2009. There are also casts of the Ardley tracks on the front lawn of the OUMNH.

Megalosaurus was William Buckland's first scalp in a personal Oxfordshire prehistoric portfolio that went on to include the flying reptile *Rhamphorynchus bucklandii*, and the Jurassic mammal *Phascolotherium bucklandii*, also known as the Stonesfield Mammal, after the village quarry where it was discovered. Phascolotherium was a night-hunter, resembling the modern-day possum. It appears to be a common ancestor of all types of mammal found on earth today.

THE PREHISTORIC UNIVERSITY

That's Hawking and Dawkins dealt with. Meanwhile, the *real* history of Oxfordshire begins with the first people. And yet we search in vain for a tidy human beginning, an Adam-and-Eve-type origins story.

It's therefore tempting to fall into the comforting arms of folklore. Writing nearly 900 years before viral Fake News came along to undermine our efforts to understand the world around us, historian Geoffrey of Monmouth wrote an epic British pseudo-history in which King Brutus, grandson of King Priam of Troy, lands on the shores of a Giant-inhabited island around 1100 BC, polishes off its small population, and renames it Britain. Brutus founds a university at Lechlade, which, three generations later, is relocated to the city of Caer Memphric, aka Oxford.

This city was founded by King Mempricius. He was an out and out rotter, Oxford's original villain, spurning his queen for a string of male lovers and killing anyone who got in his way. Thank goodness, then, that he was eaten by wolves during a badly planned hunting trip, at some point around 1010 BC.

All of which, sadly can be written off as Geoffrey of Monmouth's attempt to give his employers at Oxford University an untouchable pedigree. He was simply telling them what they wanted to hear – that Oxford's place at the heart of academia went further back than any other city's.

So, folklore only offers brief, romantic respite from the pressing issue of where Oxfordshire's human history begins. Instead, as my proper starting point, I'm turning to a far more grounded and inspiring Oxfordshire origin, one that does away with the need for meteorites, dinosaurs, fossils and folklore.

So, in the beginning there was ...

THE RIDGEWAY

This was the first thoroughfare of the region, a natural highway that makes use of the chalk escarpment of the Chilterns, the M40 of its day. It was the Ridgeway that brought people to, from and through this portion of the island – an inroad into the human story.

With the final meltdown of the Ice Age 12,000 years ago, the chalk ridge would have been poking up from the damp valleys, as inviting as a sturdy bridge over a muddy river. If you were heading this way, the Ridgeway was the only road in the county, being a thoroughfare, a vantage point, and a comforting certainty in a world of wilderness and unknowns. It was also the only route on which you could keep your feet dry at all times of the year.

The ancient pathway follows the chalk ridge in Wiltshire, Oxfordshire and Buckinghamshire. It runs parallel to part of a prehistoric routeway called the Icknield Way, named after the British tribe the Iceni. This sits lower down on the north side of the chalk escarpment, part of a road that runs for over 360 miles from Lyme Regis in Dorset to Hunstanton in Norfolk. Quite why the Icknield Way avoids the ready-made path on the chalk ridge is a mystery.

Transport through the ages: view of the M40 from the Ridgeway.

Natural historian Robert Plot wrote in 1677:

> It is called by its old name at very many places, Ikenildway, to this
> very day. Some indeed call it Icknil, some Acknil, others Hackney,
> and some again Hackington, but all intend the very same way,
> that stretches itself in this County from North-east to South-west;
> coming into it (out of Bucks) at the Parish of Chinnor, and going
> out again over the Thames (into Berks) at the Parish of Goring ...
> it passes through no town or village in the county, but only Goring;
> nor does it (as I hear) scarce anywhere else, for which reason 'tis
> much used by stealers of cattle.

It was this road that brought people to this part of the
world in the first place, a soon as the ice receded. The driving force behind early settlement was probably flint. Most
of Oxfordshire is just a stone's throw – preferably one
shaped into an axe- or arrow-head – from abundant supplies; and the mother of all flint supplies lay at the northern
end of the Icknield Way, at Grimes Graves in Norfolk.

Oxfordshire's chief Palaeolithic flints – the earliest human litter in the area – have been unearthed at Rotherfield Peppard, Berinsfield, Iffley, Crowmarsh, Benson, Ewelme, Stanton Harcourt, Cassington, Goring, and Wolvercote and Osney in Oxford. See how long you can look at them in their Ashmolean and Woodstock Museum of Oxfordshire display cases before glazing over.

OUT WITH THE OLD, IN WITH THE NEW STONE AGE

Neolithic (New Stone Age) settlers displaced the aboriginal peoples of the area more than 5,000 years ago. They built the first permanent settlements and followed an agricultural rather than hunter-gatherer way of life (including the earliest crops, livestock and extensive forest clearance). They also made pots in rudimentary kilns, and expanded on the tool portfolio by adding wood, bone and other rocks to the traditional all-purpose flint.

The Neolithic settlers erected monoliths and stone circles such as the Rollright Stones and The Devil's Quoits near Stanton Harcourt, and engineered high-tech burials involving long barrows. The Neolithic long barrow checklist includes one of the finest in the island – Wayland's Smithy near Ashbury. There are other examples in the county – although none as impressive as Wayland's – including one at Shipton and a reconstruction at Ascott-under-Wychwood.

This all predates the earliest 'Celtic' settlers of the Iron Age. It's possible that we have a fleeting glimpse of these earlier peoples in fairy stories of strong, short-statured, loyal but vengeful goblins who help around the house and farm but easily take offence, at which point they become vengeful monsters. In Oxfordshire folklore the fairy presence is limited to a few desultory sightings at Neolithic monuments such as Wayland's Smithy and the Rollright Stones, where they were last glimpsed in the late nineteenth century. (The association is celebrated with a wooden sculpture of three dancing fairies, erected at Rollright in 2017 by sculptors David and Adam Gosling. Like the original fairies, the sculpture is temporary, but should withstand the elements long enough for visitors to get a glimpse within half a dozen years of this book's publication date.)

In the 1960s fourteen bodies were unearthed at Wayland's Smithy. Recently dated to the mid-fourth century BC, they appear to be the remains of war victims. Skewered by arrows, dismembered by dogs or wild animals, they were later gathered up and buried at the site. This all suggests that the Neolithic era was every bit as violent as the ages that followed.

THE STORY OF TRACING BEAKERS

At some point between 2000 and 1500 BC, settlers from the Rhineland and the north coast of Europe – the Belgic people, from modern Netherlands and Belgium – arrived. Their calling card in the archaeological record is a distinctive bell-shaped beaker, which has led to the period being dubbed the Beaker or Bell-Beaker culture. As far as we know, the Beaker Folk settled peaceably, but we can only speculate. There is no evidence of war or displacement, but these things are not always obvious in the archaeology; and the previously cited evidence of a massacre at Wayland's Smithy hints at the possible truth.

The bell-beaker was the smartphone of its day, sweeping all before it as a cultural calling card, and probably rendering the pre-Beaker resident indistinguishable from the invader. We tend to view these things through the blood-tinted spectacles of nation and empire, but the prehistoric period was more about sparse populations of traders and distant cousins. It's a pre-British natural history of the human species, rather than a tribal battleground. Think David Attenborough rather than Richard Starkey.

There is no distinct boundary between the Neolithic and the Bronze Age; nor, indeed, between the Bronze and Iron Ages. The Beaker Folk traded bronze goods with their neighbours in what is now Ireland. The metal was either imported from the European mainland, or recast by local bronzesmiths recycling old or broken objects. One of the oldest bronze artefacts surviving from this period is a cauldron unearthed at Shipton-on-Cherwell, on display with other artefacts from the era in Oxford's Ashmolean Museum.

THE ORIGINAL IRON MAN

Iron tools first appeared in Oxfordshire in the sixth century BC. Iron ore seams in the north of the region were mined for the raw materials, although most of the ironmongery was imported from elsewhere. Iron working was both an art and a science, and the smiths behind the alchemy of transmuting rock to metal weapon were viewed as no less than magicians.

This notion of smith-as-wonderworker is captured in the folklore of Wayland's Smithy. The name is Saxon, a down-at-heel version of the Germanic and Scandinavian smith-god Weland/Völundr. Legend says that Wayland will nail horseshoes to the feet of any unshod steed tethered at the long barrow, if a payment is left.

Oxfordshire's hillforts date from the Bronze and Iron Ages. These constructions were a mixture of cattle and sheep corrals and defensive forts in the modern sense of the word. The best surviving one is at Uffington Castle. It was occupied for hundreds of years, the earliest version having appeared in the ninth century BC. Sitting beside Dragon Hill, with its livid battle scars of chalk, and the iconic Uffington White Horse, this is a foremost pilgrimage spot for ancient history buffs.

The White Horse itself, disjointed like bones in a plundered grave, has been the object of legend, speculation and logo inspiration for as long as humans have gazed on it. The figure was carved into the hillside no earlier than 1200 BC, possibly as late as the sixth century BC, and has been renovated regularly ever since. Scouring the White Horse became a local fair-cum-festival in the sixteenth century, held every seven years, and is celebrated in *Tom Brown's Schooldays* author Thomas Hughes' rambling memoir *The Scouring of the White Horse* (1859). The event is also mythologised in G.K. Chesterton's poem about Alfred the Great, *The Ballad of the White Horse* (1911):

> *And it fell in the days of Alfred,*
> *In the days of his repose,*
> *That as old customs in his sight*
> *Were a straight road and a steady light,*
> *He bade them keep the White Horse white*

As the first plume of the snows.
And right to the red torchlight,
From the trouble of morning grey,
They stripped the White Horse of the grass
As they strip it to this day.

The Horse is still 'scoured' regularly, by teams of volunteers from the National Trust. The only time it has been hidden from view was in the Second World War, when it was covered in foliage to conceal it from Luftwaffe bombers on the lookout for geographical landmarks.

Folklore insists that the horse is actually a dragon, and not just any old dragon but the one killed by St George. The chalk 'scars' on neighbouring Dragon Hill were burned into the ground by the dragon's spilled blood. But another folkloric strand maintains that the horse is indeed equine, and that it leaves the hillside at night to graze on the hillslope and valley bottom, known as The Manger.

Other hillforts survive at Madmarston, Ilbury, Idbury, Wyfold, Binditch and the Dyke Hills near Dorchester. Madmarston was occupied for at least 250 years (up to *c.* AD 50), with three banks and a ditch, as well-defended as any castle. This lengthy occupation suggests that the fort was a town of sorts, the HQ of a local tribe. The forts survive as sulky mounds in fields attacked by plough and sheep – still besieged after all these centuries.

We tend to call all the post-Beaker Folk inhabitants of the island Celtic. This is not a tag the people would have recognised themselves, however. The earlier settlers of Oxfordshire spoke a language related to modern Irish and Scottish; the later waves, arriving between AD 500 and 400, spoke the Brythonic language. The linguistic descendants of this tongue still flourish in modern Welsh and Cornish.

FIRST CENTURY BC:
IT'S GRIM DOWN SOUTH

The first local tribe to bequeath its name to history (via the Romans) was the Catuvellauni. Originally from the Low Countries, these people had established a kingdom centred on Camulodunum (Colchester). Marching west – following the sun, as settlers always have – the incoming army would have invaded via the Ridgeway. Or perhaps they bribed, threatened and traded their way in, which is a method of invasion and cultural conquest very much at the forefront of international relations today. The evidence of their presence – or influence – is in coins and pottery.

The Catuvellauni seem to have made it as far west as the River Cherwell. On the opposite side of the river, the coin evidence suggests that other tribes were dominant, including the Dobunni (based in what later became Gloucestershire). The bank and ditch structure known as Grim's Ditch, spanning the fields between the rivers Glyme and Windrush, is evidence that one faction wanted to build walls to keep out the 'foreigners' (sound familiar?); but it is not clear whether it was the non-Catuvellaunis trying to hold back the easterners, or the Catuvellauni themselves making a stand against the later Roman invaders.

Then again, the structure – like the other Grim's Ditch at the southern end of the county – may have been more of an administrative boundary. The boring answer is often the correct one in history.

ROMANO-BRITAIN
43 BC–AD 450

Julius Caesar crossed the Thames near Wallingford en route to a battle against the Britons at Cirencester in 54 BC. That particular invasion ended in defeat for the Romans; but they made it to Oxfordshire a few years after their first successful occupation of the island in AD 43 during the reign of Emperor Claudius.

As they crossed the country from the south-east coast into the west, the Romans constructed the road Akeman Street. It enters Oxfordshire at the village of Blackthorn, and exits west of Shilton. Another road, running north–south between Silchester in Hampshire and Towcester in Northamptonshire, linked the Roman towns of Dorchester-on-Thames and Alchester, the two roads forming a crossroads at the latter town.

This north–south road, a Roman army supply line, crossed Otmoor, with foundations of brushwood to keep it from sinking in the wet ground. Elsewhere the roads were up to 25 ft wide and paved. Our old friends the Ridgeway and Icknield Way were paved in places too during the Roman era.

Alchester (the site of which is in modern Wendlebury, near Bicester) was the earliest Roman town in the area, smothering an older British settlement and developing in the shadow of an earlier Roman fort at Little Chesterton. The fort was built around AD 45 to house the Second Augustan Legion, instrumental in the conquest of Britain, under the command of future Roman emperor Vespasian (AD 9–79). The site was a strategic military spot between the British Catuvellauni and the Dobunni tribes who, like all the pre-Roman Iron Age tribes of the island, were in a constant face-off. The legion moved out in AD 68, and Alchester became a comfy Romano-British town, until its abandonment in the fifth century AD.

THE FIRST LOCALS

One Alchester resident's tombstone was unearthed in 2003, bearing the name Lucius Valerius Geminus, an Italian-born veteran of the Legio II. In translation, the stone reads:

> To the souls of the departed: Lucius Valerius Geminus, the son of Lucius, of the Pollia voting tribe, from Forum Germanorum, veteran of the Second Augustan Legion, aged 50, lies here. His heir had this set up in accordance with his will.

Lucius' links to the legion place his death in the mid to latter part of the first century AD. This makes him Oxfordshire's earliest named resident. The stone is on display in the Museum of Oxfordshire, Woodstock.

Three quarters of a century later, a Romano-British pot maker, the second oldest known Oxfordshire native, left his mark on posterity. Dated to around AD 150, a fragment of pot formerly kept in the Museum of Oxford reads TΛ·MII·SV·BV·GVS·FII· – or *Tamesubugus Fe[cit]*, as it is usually rendered, as those double 'I's represented an 'E', apparently. The name probably means 'Thames Dweller'.

There have been other theories about the meaning of 'Tamesubugus', however. The 'bugus' element could mean breaker or striker, or even 'blue', rather than dweller. Experts all agree on the incomplete word 'fecit', meaning 'made this', based on conventions inferred from similar inscriptions. So, the fragment is declaring 'Thames Dweller made this' ... probably.

Oxfordshire's second big Roman town after Alchester was Dorchester-on-Thames (occupied around AD 70 on the site of a pre-Roman settlement). This settlement has bequeathed us another early resident. Third century AD tax collector Marcus Vatrius Severus erected an altar here dedicated to Jupiter and the Emperor-as-God. Unfortunately, the altar disappeared in the early twentieth century, sold for a guinea (£1.05) shortly after being unearthed.

ROMANO-WHO?

There were other Roman roads in the area, laid for practical and commercial rather than military purposes, including one that stretched north-east to south-west, from Bicester to Wantage. Other major towns in this period included Frilford, a thriving centre before the Romans arrived. Remains of temples and an amphitheatre have been found here.

All of which begs the question: who exactly were the people living in Roman Oxfordshire? Roman Britain wasn't full of people from Italy (in spite of the Italian origins of our first-named resident Lucius, mentioned previously). Ninety-nine per cent of the locals were the Brythonic Celtic people whose ancestors had been here since those tribes began occupying the island after AD 500. This is the population we now label 'Romano-British', although that tag should only by applied to town dwellers, who were living a life influenced, fuelled and financed by the Roman social structure and economy. Most of the locals still lived in the simple mud, straw and wood huts of their distant ancestors.

There would have been 'foreign' residents too, mainly army retirees and other officials; but most of these would have been from parts of the Roman Empire neighbouring Britain, not the environs of Rome itself.

The more enterprising businessmen, mainly in the north of the county near Akeman Street, grew wheat and other crops to feed the ravenous Roman forts and towns. Chieftains of the Dobunni and Catuvellauni tribes soon became rich on this gravy train, and every bit as 'Roman' as the retired consuls and army generals next door. In this we can see the earliest roots of the inherent racial otherness of the British aristocracy. Previously, British kings and chieftains, although probably elevated to the level of sub-gods, had been essentially local, 'one of us', a sturdy branch of the native land. But from now on, marital links and allegiances to a ruling caste – in this case Roman – set apart the genealogy, self-image and preferred language of 'Romano-British' leaders and landowners from those who were simply British.

In later centuries this trend would continue, with royalty speaking French (and later still, German) at court, the educated folk still conversing in Latin, and the peasantry conversing in whichever language – British, Old

English, Emoji – the changing times had bequeathed them.

It was this increasing reliance on Roman identity, assistance and influence that would prove the downfall of the warring British tribes after the implosion of the Roman Empire in the fifth century.

INVISIBLE OXFORD

Oxfordshire was not the site of any large-scale Roman industry, but there were several utilitarian suppliers such as pot makers. These clung to the main roads, for trading purposes, with imitation Samian ware tossed off at Sandford-on-Thames, and a busy pottery at Cowley, up and running at the end of the first century AD. It remained in use for almost 200 years, with other thriving kilns in the Oxford area, at Rose Hill, Headington, and the vicinity of the Churchill Hospital, long before the foundation of the city.

That's one of the odd things about Oxford. There were satellite settlements and cottage industries, and later there were religious communities too, but Oxford itself stubbornly refuses to emerge until that first documented mention of it in the year 912.

Most of the Roman villas of the period seem to have been built north of Akeman Street. The most tourist-friendly remains, however, are at North Leigh near Witney (kept by English Heritage). This villa grew over the years to become one of the largest in the island. The surviving highlight is a magnificent third-century mosaic floor.

The survival of this floor is something to be thankful for, given the treatment of the mosaic unearthed at a fourth-century villa in nearby Stonesfield. The pavement, featuring Bacchus riding on a panther, was uncovered in 1712, sketched in great detail, and then argued over and eventually destroyed by the disgruntled tenant on whose land it had been discovered. It was covered, and later lost altogether under the plough.

Ditchley near Charlbury had a fine villa too, built where Ditchley House stands today. A Roman hoard was discovered nearby in 1934, containing 1,176 bronze coins. They range in date over a 100-year period from AD 270 onwards, and are thought to have been buried in their ceramic pot around AD 395, at a time when the Romano-British were getting increasingly jumpy about the decline of their spiritual homeland in Rome. The hoard can be viewed in the Ashmolean in Oxford.

Smaller villas existed further south, including ones at Beckley and Harpsden near Henley, but in general Roman Oxfordshire is marked by a south–north divide.

BY JOVE!

We know that the pre-Roman and Romano-British folk had their own religions, but they are largely unknowable. We don't have the creed, the rituals or the mindset to give us much more than a shadow of a ghost of a clue. There are writings about mainstream Roman deities and practices, but nothing to tell us what local religious and ritual quirks the Oxfordshire Romano-Britons were into.

Woodeaton seems to have been a place of preeminent religious significance, as witnessed by the many coins and votive offerings found there at the site of a Roman temple. This was built on top of an even older temple, and the discovery of pretend-bronze axe heads and bird figurines – a selection of them can be seen in the Ashmolean Museum – shows that people were communing here with something or other. The place remained a pilgrimage site after the Romans had departed, and the current church is on this same site. But as to who these local deities were, it's guesswork. Gods and goddesses have always moved in mysterious ways.

Nothing lasts for long. The next turning point in Britain came in AD 383 when Roman legions abandoned Hadrian's Wall, leaving the Picts, Scots and northern British tribes to fight it out (something that continued for the next 1,000 years). In Oxfordshire, though, the experience of crumbling Roman authority would have first manifested itself not with incursions of northern Celts, but with Germanic soldiers. As Roman martial might took to its boats and abandoned the island, Romano-British kings looked to mercenary armies to take their place and protect them from the increasingly ambitious Picts and Irish-Scots, who began raiding from the north and west.

The German and Frisian coasts had plenty of willing mercenaries, and Britain soon had its next influx of economic migrants – the Anglo-Saxons.

THE ANGLO-SAXON AND DANISH ERA
450–1066

In the year 407, Rome officially withdrew its troops from Britain. Things went downhill rapidly for the would-be inheritors of the mess left behind, with Scots and Picts penetrating into the midlands and the south, this time looking to extend their own kingdoms, not just take home a few spoils of war.

Some British chieftains invited mercenaries over from northern Europe, to act as household guards and personal armies. These mercenaries soon invited their kinsmen across the Channel – Angles, Saxons, Jutes and Frisians, many from what is now Schleswig-Holstein on the German–Denmark border.

In Oxfordshire, the Roman villas were abandoned and the Roman roads were soon thick with weeds. The only ones that survived the decay ran from Bicester to Towcester, and Bicester to Aylesbury. Stratton Audley is named after a surviving Roman 'street', which became part of the parish boundary.

There is not much continuity between the Roman settlements and the Anglo-Saxon ones that followed.

Alchester, which had been the main Roman town, was abandoned altogether. Dorchester bucked the trend, and the incoming hordes settled there. This settling had begun under the Romano-British leaders, who had hired Anglo-Saxon armies to guard the town soon after the withdrawal of the Roman army. The graves of these proto-Saxons have been found in the town, predating the main Anglo-Saxon invasions by some fifty years. When the invading army finally arrived, Dorchester was their first settlement, presumably because there was a warm welcome for them there.

BYE BYE BRITAIN

According to local legend, Ambrosden is named after Romano-British king Ambrosius Aurelianus. He rallied the various Celtic tribes and succeeded in winning back the island from the invading Saxons in the first half of the fifth century AD. Treacherously poisoned, he passed the crown to his brother Uther Pendragon, who in turn handed it down to his son – Ambrosius' nephew – King Arthur.

Ambrosius is from the one period of British history that truly counts as a Dark Age: the chronicle-free transition from Roman Britain to Anglo-Saxon England. He seems to have existed, but the links to Arthur are later wishful thinking; and Ambrosden itself is probably not named after the warlord king at all, but from Saxon elements meaning 'Ambre's Hill'.

The pseudo-historical Celtic backlash led by shadowy figures such as Arthur and Ambrosius did not last long. The Saxon mercenaries defeated their former employers and drove back the Picts and Scots too. As ever, conquest was 99 per cent cultural and 1 per cent visceral. There was a change of leadership and language, and therefore social order, rather than a physical, body-for-body replacement of Britons by Saxons. Genetic tests in the early twenty-first century confirmed what historians had always suspected – that the average 'English' stock of modern rural Middle England is, genetically speaking, still largely pre-Roman British.

Nowhere was this more true than in Oxfordshire, far inland from the coasts where the invaders were making their first permanent settlements. The invaders trickled in along the Icknield Way in the east, and eventually from the south and south-west too. Pagan, proto-English culture seeped through the land like ground frost, and Oxfordshire soon found itself in a love–hate sandwich between the kingdoms of Wessex to the south and Mercia to the north.

Much of Oxfordshire remained more Romano-British than Anglo-Saxon, until later in the sixth century. Saxon Cuthwulf's victories against the British at Benson and Eynsham in 571 proved to be the point of no return for the Britons. Cuthwulf gave the land to his brother Ceawlin, king of a Saxon tribe called the Gewisse. A royal Mercian court was set up at Benson, and by 584 the Gewisse had conquered most of southern Oxfordshire, with their main base at Dorchester. Their land was later soaked up by the kingdom of Wessex.

Local legend says that Cuthwulf was killed in one of the battles, and buried in a barrow called Cuthwulf's Low, now known as Cutteslowe, a suburb of Oxford. This barrow was levelled in 1261, as it had become a notorious meeting place for robbers and ne'er do wells.

South Oxfordshire was in Saxon hands, and north Oxfordshire soon capitulated. Seventeenth-century natural historian Robert Plot wrote:

> For eminent places in this county, during the government of the Saxons and Danes in Britain, we may reckon first Banbury ... where Kenric, the second West-Saxon King, about the Year 556 put to flight the Britons, fighting for their lives, estates, and all they had.

The Anglo-Saxons completed their conquest of north Oxfordshire in the early seventh century. In 613 the final round of Saxons-versus-Britons took place near Bampton, where warlords Cwichelm and Cynegils boasted of slaying more than 2,000 enemy soldiers.

An Anglo-Saxon tribe called the Hwicce gave their name to Wychwood Forest, although the bulk of their land lay in modern Gloucestershire and Worcestershire. The dominant force in the north of Oxfordshire was Mercia, which remained the preeminent Saxon kingdom for many decades before the arrival of the Danish invaders, who whittled away at its power to the north and east while Wessex grew in stature to the south. Oxfordshire was trapped in this power struggle like a beach washed by two seas at once.

In 752 the West Saxons rose up against their overlords the Mercians at the Battle of Burford. After a long and bloody conflict, Wessex king Cuthred defeated Mercian king Aethelbald and took the latter's golden dragon banner as a trophy of his victory. The battle took place on land still known as Battle Edge, beside Sheep Street. A stone sarcophagus, found on the site and presumed to belong to a leading participant in the conflict, sits near the West Gate of Burford churchyard.

Benson was probably the site of the Battle of Bensington in 779, when Wessex king Cynewulf, son of the victorious Cuthred, was defeated by king Offa of Mercia, who annexed Berkshire to his kingdom as a prize.

THAT OLD TIME RELIGION

While the north of the county was being shaped by Mercians, Dorchester and the south underwent radical change in 635 when the pope-sanctioned Frankish missionary Birinus converted the Gewisse tribe to Christianity. Their king Cynegils was baptised, and the diocese of Dorchester was established – one of the oldest in England. Birinus was its first bishop, dying there in 650.

Birinus established many other churches too, having made it his mission to Christianise pagan Wessex. It wasn't all plain sailing, though, and Cynegils' son Cenwalh refused to turn away from his old Germanic gods. He married the daughter of his pagan neighbour King Penda of Mercia, but was forced into exile in East Anglia when he abandoned her. Cenwalh finally succumbed to baptism there; but he remained Saxon to the core. When he became king he spoke out against Agilbert, second Bishop of Dorchester, on the grounds that he was a foreigner. Agilbert left the country in disgust in 660, and Cenwalh installed a Saxon called Wine, the first to be titled Bishop of Winchester. Dorchester was swallowed by Mercia after Cenwalh's reign, and remained a powerful diocese until 1072, when the Normans moved the bishopric of this enormous see to Lincoln.

Edwold, brother of East Anglian king Edmund, turned down the offer of that kingdom's crown when Edmund was murdered by the Danes in 869. Instead, he chose to retire to the monastic community at Dorchester.

The other major religious events of the early Saxon period were the founding of Abingdon Abbey in 675, and St Frideswide's Abbey in 727. These were both rebuilt and refounded in the eleventh century. Eynsham had a minster in the eighth century too, refounded as an abbey in 1005. It was abandoned in 1066, but repopulated in the later eleventh century.

Abingdon Abbey was founded by Cissa, the viceroy of Centwine, King of Wessex, and enjoyed the patronage of Wessex kings until Danish soldiers broke down its walls and plundered its riches in the 870s. King Alfred managed to drive the Danes from the area, after a long and arduous war, but the monks were apparently not sufficiently grateful for this, as Alfred afterwards closed the abbey and confiscated its lands. It rose from the ashes in the tenth century, and remained a major religious institution until 1538 when it was knocked down as part of the dissolution of the monasteries.

Frideswide (650–727) was daughter of King Didan of Eynsham, and is said to have founded a monastery or priory on the site of modern Christ Church College in Oxford. It was rebuilt in the twelfth century, and Christ Church Cathedral is a relic of that foundation. It is very possible that this foundation marks the beginnings of the city of Oxford, as it is close to the original 'oxen ford' over the Thames. There were certainly people living in the area around modern St Aldate's at this time. However, there is no mention of Oxford by name.

Frideswide's Christian parents Didan and Sefrida ruled a region equivalent to modern-day Berkshire and southwest Oxfordshire, and gave their daughter the land and money to found her monastery. According to legend, she was very beautiful, and captivated neighbouring Mercian king Algar. He asked for her hand in marriage, and when she refused, citing her vow of celibacy and the fact that Algar was a pagan, he attempted to abduct her. Frideswide fled to Binsey – or Frilsham in Berkshire, according to some versions of the legend – and took shelter with a swineherd. He allowed her to look after his pigs, and she laid low for three years before returning to her monastery.

Algar then reappeared, threatening to burn everything down and have his wicked way with Frideswide. Before he could achieve these dubious goals, there was a flash of lightning, and Algar was blinded. Frideswide made him swear that he would stop chasing her, and after accepting his promise she returned to her life as an abbess, giving warning that henceforth any king who attempted to enter the city with violent intent would suffer the same fate as Algar – the so-called Curse of St Frideswide. For complying with these terms, Algar was given back his sight.

Frideswide's fame was a magnet for donations to the priory, which soon became rich. She ended her days back in Binsey, founding a nunnery and causing a magical holy well to spring forth (the still-flowing Treacle Well). She died there in 727, and was made a saint some 400 years later.

OXFORD CALLING

According to the anonymous author of the Abingdon Chronicle (part of the Anglo-Saxon Chronicle), in the year 912:

> This year died Æthered ealdorman of the Mercians, and King
> Edward took possession of London and Oxford and of all the lands
> which owed obedience thereto.

This is the first definite mention of Oxford, although it was clearly an established city by that point, otherwise Æthered would have had nothing to take possession of. This gives us a foundation for the city in the reign of King Alfred's son Edward the Elder (AD 899–912) at the very latest; but probably much earlier, at the time of St Frideswide's abbey's fame in the later eighth century, or in the reign of King Alfred. Historians have found this latter idea very appealing over the years, but it should be emphasised that there is no hard evidence, just wild flights of logic and common sense.

Oxford's surviving buildings give no support to the pre-King Edward hypotheses. Its oldest surviving building is the mid-eleventh-century St Michael's church tower. A mix of the holy and the secular, the structure has functioned as a watchtower on the North Gate of the city walls, and was formerly attached to the city's Bocardo Prison.

The layout of the original city suggests a fortified town, a grid-like structure based on the crossroads at Carfax. It has been suggested that this is the result of fortification during the era of Danish invasion.

The lack of firm evidence did not prevent University College from claiming King Alfred the Great as its founder. They settled on the year 872 as the foundation, and duly celebrated their thousandth birthday in June 1872. Even at the time it was widely accepted that the Alfred link, for all its plausibility and possibility, has no basis in written records. So, the college will have to celebrate its thousandth birthday for a second time, in the year 2249.

(Abingdon School did this trick the other way around: in 1963 it celebrated its 400th anniversary, and in 2006 it celebrated its 750th. This is because they formerly traced its establishment to 1563, which was actually its re-foundation date. The current hierarchy takes the earliest mention of the institution, in an Abingdon Abbey charter of 1256, as the starting point. But many historians believe the whole thing started earlier still, citing a document from 1100 that mentions an Abingdon headmaster.)

The first death in Oxford is recorded in the Abingdon Chronicle for the year AD 924:

> This year King Edward died among the Mercians at Farndon; and very shortly, about sixteen days after this, Elward his son died at Oxford; and their bodies lie at Winchester.

With the city came the suburbs. St Clements was settled in the tenth century, as was the Osney Island area, and the land to the north of the city around St Mary Magdalen Church and St Giles.

DANISH PASTING

There is no seamless transition between the Anglo-Saxon era and the Danish era. In the south of the island, the action began in 865 when a huge Viking fleet dubbed the Great Heathen Army, led by Ivar the Boneless, made landfall in East Anglia, with a plan to conquer all the kingdoms of the Anglo-Saxons – East Anglia, Northumbria, Wessex and Mercia.

Mercia faced the music three years later, and 21-year-old King Æthelred I (who had one of his royal courts at Woodstock) and his Wantage-born younger brother Alfred led the Saxons against the Danish army. In 870 the invaders had beaten them back to Wessex, and there were nine battles over the following twelve months. The initial outcome was stalemate.

ALFRED THE GREAT BLOWS IT

The Battle of Ashdown took place on 8 January 871. The Danes, under King Bagsecg, fresh from victory against the Saxons at Reading, marched to Ashdown to meet the forces of Æthelred and Alfred. The Danes had the advantage of arms and experience, but the Saxons had potentially more men – as long as they could summon them in the first place.

According to legend, the young prince Alfred rode to Blowingstone Hill at Kingston Lisle and blew a rallying blast from the natural rock feature called the Blowing Stone. Only a skilled player could get a note out of this unprom-ising sarsen stone instrument, and only a man born to be king could make it heard across the surrounding downs as far as White Horse Hill. The locals came racing to Alfred's side, and the ensuing Battle of Ashdown was a victory for the Saxons, with King Bagsecg and his chief earls slain.

The Blowing Stone has survived the centuries, but is now at the foot of Blowingstone Hill, in a private garden. Kingstanding Hill near Moulsford is also associated with the Ashdown campaign – it was here that Alfred encamped and, presumably, stood.

Victory was short-lived. A few weeks later, the Saxon army was defeated at the Battle of Basing in Hampshire, and again a month later at the Battle of Merton (proba-bly Marden in Wiltshire). King Æthelred died, probably as a result of battle wounds, on 23 April 871, and young Alfred became king.

In the following years Alfred suffered serious defeats, eventually reduced to hiding in the Somerset marshes and apocryphally burning cakes. But he still managed to turn the tide, and the wars finally ceased when he beat Danish king Guthrum to a standstill at the Battle of Ethandun in Wiltshire, in the year 878, paving the way for the treaty of partition that created the Danelaw in the north of the island. This gave the Danes most of the island, but it ensured the survival of Wessex, which included Wantage, Wallingford and a decent chunk of Oxfordshire within its boundaries. The rest of the county was under the rule of King Guthrum the Dane.

Alfred was a regular visitor to Oxfordshire during his reign, and there is a local tradition in Shifford that he held one of the first all-England parliaments there in 885, with 'many Thanes, many Bishops, and many learned Men, wise Earls, and Knights'. A surviving patch of land called Court Close in Shifford is supposed to commemorate Alfred's parliament.

Until the mid-nineteenth century it was an accepted fact that Alfred had strong associations with Oxford. In 1869 local historian John Davenport could declare without blushing:

Alfred the Great and His three Sons long resided in Oxford; and, it is believed, in a Castle, with a Keep Tower (built by Offa, King of Mercia), on part of the future site of the Oxford Castle ... Alfred also resided in the Manor House, or Palace, at Woodstock, and there translated Boethius. Alfred is the reputed Founder, in the year 872, of University College, Oxford. Certain it is that He gave life to the then nucleus of an University. He built three Colleges, or Halls. The first for Grammar, situate near the East Gate of the City ... called Parva Universitatis Aula; the second for logic and philosophy, to which Alfred gave the name of Aula minor Universitatis. This Hall was in School Street, a site now forming part of Brasenose College. And the third Hall was for Divinity Students, and occupied part of the larger quadrangle of the present University College; and this Alfred called Aula magna Universitatis.

Sadly, there is evidence for none of this – apart from the bit about Woodstock.

OXFORD MASSACRE AND COUNTER-MASSACRE

King Edward the Elder, Alfred's son, reigned from 899 to 924. He was the man who first drew the county boundaries in Wessex, including Berkshire and Oxfordshire. His intention was to create highly organised defensive areas, enabling the Anglo-Saxons to face down the still-restless Danes. Hook Norton is mentioned as one of the victims of rekindled hostilities, razed by Danes in 914.

But by 916 Edward had pretty much succeeded in his aims of driving the Vikings from Mercia, with just a few Danish landowning Jarls allowed to remain and with a sizeable ghetto in Oxford. He was assisted in his mission by his pugilistic sister Æthelflæd, fondly titled Lady of the Mercians. The reverberations of their victories travelled north and inspired a new Saxon resistance movement, and in 954 the last of the Danelaw kings, Eric Bloodaxe, was driven from York.

Edward's successor Æthelstan (894–939) was the first man to use the title King of England – quite an achievement after the civil wars that had shaped his youth. This marked the end of Wessex, Mercia and the other kingdoms. England was now a single unit consisting of administrative units, including one called Oxfordshire. Wessex now existed as a royal house title (like Tudor, Stuart and Windsor in the centuries to come).

Oxfordshire thrived under Æthelstan, who lived at one point in Oxford and held at least one Witan (council) at Dorchester-on-Thames. However, a generation later the old truces and alliances were crumbling. New waves of Danes arrived on the east coast in the 980s, and after their victory at the Battle of Maldon in 991, 22-year-old King Æthelred II was forced to pay a tribute, called Danegeld, to the Danish throne.

Æthelred's nickname was 'the Unready', meaning 'uncounselled'. This was meant to be a joke, as the name Æthelred means 'well counselled'. Uncounselled or otherwise, he had many bases in Oxfordshire, including Eynsham, Headington, Islip, Oxford and Woodstock.

In a theme all too familiar from modern politics, Æthelred was a headstrong ruler who followed his own impulses, passions and prejudices. His classic piece of uncounselled action came in the year 1002 when he reasserted English dominance by ordering reprisals against the old enemy, the Danes. They had, he said, 'sprung like weeds among the wheat'. He encouraged his subjects to stage pogroms on St Brice's Day, 13 November, the traditional time of year for bull-baiting and the slaughtering of livestock. Æthelred hoped to catch his people in a bloodthirsty mood.

In Oxford the king's call to arms was taken up enthusiastically, and the local Danes, vastly outnumbered, fled for their lives to the sanctuary of St Frideswide's church on the site of modern Christ Church Cathedral. The Saxons torched the building, mopping up with their swords and arrows any Dane who tried to flee, or who had failed to hole up in the church.

Historian John of Wallingford, who died in 1258, wrote about the Oxford massacre in a chronicle covering the period 449 to 1036. Amongst his insights was the revelation that one of the sources of resentment against the Danes was their good personal hygiene:

> The Danes, thanks to their habit of combing their hair every day, of bathing every Saturday and regularly changing their clothes, were able to undermine the virtue of married women and even seduce the daughters of nobles to be their mistresses.

In other words, the smelly Saxons became jealous of their neighbours' amorous conquests, and took drastic action.

There is an alternative version of the story. Oxford, it is said, was the venue for a treaty-signing session between Danish generals Sigeferth and Morkere and Saxon ealdorman Eadric. The Viking guests were butchered during supper, and it was their avenging army that managed to get itself cornered and roasted in St Frideswide's.

The St Brice's Day Massacre was the stuff of largely unsubstantiated legend until 2010 when a mass grave at St John's College on St Giles in Oxford was unearthed, containing the bones of thirty-odd violently terminated Danes. St Giles isn't very close to Christ Church, but the bodies had been dumped in a ditch, probably a mass grave to which corpses were dragged from various parts of the city. The skeletons had an assortment of cracked skulls – plus one decapitee – wounds in spines and pelvic bones, and burns. The clincher came when analysis showed the bones had belonged to men who ate more fish and shellfish than the average Saxon, pointing to seafood-loving Scandinavians.

Whatever the details, this massacre inspired King Sweyn Forkbeard of Denmark, Norway and Sweden to invade England a few years later. His sister Gunnhild, kept as a hostage in Oxford as part of a former peace treaty, had been killed in the massacre and he wanted revenge. A huge Scandinavian army landed on the east coast, just like in the good old days, and slowly made its way north.

The first reprisals against Oxford came in 1009. A chronicle of the time records: '... after midwinter the Danes took an excursion up through Chiltern, and so to Oxford; which city they burned, and plundered on both sides of the Thames to their ships'.

Sweyn did not stop after this brutal revenge on Oxford, though. In 1013, after several false starts during the previous decade, he conquered the whole island. The Chronicle again:

> After he came over Watling Street, they went to Oxford, and the town-dwellers soon bowed to him, and gave hostages. From there they went to Winchester, and the people did the same, then eastward to London.

Sweyn's reign as King of England was brief – less than one year – and Æthelred even managed to reclaim the throne when he died; but his son and grandsons, Cnut, Harold I and Harthacnut, reigned for twenty-six years combined, and the kings of England remained Anglo-Danish until the Norman Conquest in 1066.

EVERYDAY LIFE IN SAXON OXFORDSHIRE

In the late tenth and early eleventh centuries, there were seven Royal Estates in Oxfordshire, based on the villages of Bampton, Bloxham, Benson, Headington, Kirtlington, Shipton-under-Wychwood and Wootton. There was a hunting lodge at Woodstock, occupying land on which Woodstock Palace and Blenheim Palace were built in later years. The other big landowners in the region were the abbey at Dorchester-on-Thames, and the abbeys at Abingdon and Eynsham.

The first Abbot of Eynsham, Ælfric (955–1014) – probably not the same man as fellow Abbot Ælfric of Abingdon, who lived around the same time – was one of the most prolific writers of his day. Most of his work is of a religious and philosophical nature, but he also left records of the ordinary life of the Eynsham peasant – from which we can infer the general lot of the peasantry at that time.

Life revolved around working the land, with ploughing in autumn and spring being particularly onerous times of year. Men would rise at dawn, yoke their oxen – in pairs, with up to eight per plough – and prepare an acre of land a day, with a boy to prod the beasts and urge them on. Nearly all the produce that resulted from these labours went to the local landowners.

The communities where these hard-pressed folk lived were small and simple – wooden framed wattle-and-daub cottages with thatched roofs, and populations of just a few dozen. The only settlements of anything approaching town-size were Oxford, Wantage, Wallingford, Banbury and Dorchester.

There were richer pickings for those who worked for the king, with men at the Woodstock hunting lodge

Fifteenth-century dovecote at Minster Lovell.

enjoying gifts of clothes, food, horses and jewellery. In the latter category, the greatest local survival from this time is the Minster Lovell Jewel, unearthed in that village in 1860. It is thought to have been made in the same workshop (in Winchester or Glastonbury) that produced the Alfred Jewel, one of the greatest surviving treasures of the Anglo-Saxon period. Both can be admired in Oxford's Ashmolean Museum.

ANGLO-SAXON TWILIGHT

According to legend, Edmund II (Ironside), son of Æthelred, and king for just seven troubled months in 1016, was murdered in Oxford, hacked to death while he was sitting on the loo. Most historians now think he died in London, but murder of some sort has not been ruled out. His successor Cnut, the son of Sweyn Forkbeard, had more success, residing in Oxford and holding many councils there between 1016 and 1035, and burning down the city for good measure in 1032.

Local legend associates Cherbury with Cnut, in the days before the Dane gained the crown. He and his men were in the village, unaware that Saxons from nearby Uffington Castle hillfort were making the 6-mile trek to Cherbury, in an attempt to ambush Cnut and drive him from the island. However, the Saxon army was spotted by a shepherd boy, who warned Cnut. The Danes marched out to meet the foe, and the two armies fought at the crossroads between Charney Bassett and Buckland. Cnut was victorious, and the site of that victory was afterwards named Gainfield.

In gratitude, Cnut gave the shepherd boy all the land within sound of his shepherd's horn when blown at Pusey. Quite how this was calculated is not recorded. The alleged horn in question, a relic known as the Pusey Horn, is in London's Victoria and Albert Museum.

Cnut's son Harold I (called Harold Harefoot on account of his great speed on the hunting field) was crowned in Oxford in 1035. His death, in Oxford on 17 March 1040, enabled his brother Harthacnut to take the throne peacefully. He had been preparing to usurp his brother, so there was probably a certain amount of relief when Harold passed away, thus avoiding another civil war.

Harold was buried at Westminster Abbey; but Harthacnut still wanted symbolic victory. He had the corpse exhumed, beheaded and dumped in a Thameside bog. Fishermen rescued it after Harthacnut's coronation, and it was buried in the main Danish cemetery in London, and later reburied at St Clement Danes in Westminster.

The cause of Harold's death is unknown. The Danes said he had been 'elf-struck' (i.e. killed by elves – an early explanation for the condition known as a stroke). Harthacnut's death two years later, after some form of seizure, suggests that there may have been a genetic propensity for strokes in the family.

EDWARD FAILS TO CONFESS

Edward the Confessor was born in Islip in 1004, in a palace built by his father Æthelred II. A thousand years later the village celebrated this fact with various events, including a ceremonial boat-burning and a visit from Channel 4's *Time Team*. The TV archaeologists endeavoured to uncover the palace and a twelfth-century chapel dedicated to the Confessor. The latter had been knocked down in the late eighteenth century, but a detailed drawing of the building had survived, and it would surely be a relatively simple feat to uncover foundations.

The dig turned up nothing – no palace, no chapel. Some stone walls unearthed at a promising site turned out to be a seventeenth-century cesspit, with preserved faeces intact.

The elusive Edward was very much the victim of turbulent times and multiple dynastic loyalties. His mother was Emma of Normandy (who had also been married to Anglo-Danish King Cnut, and was the great aunt of William the Conqueror), and his family had whisked him to safety in Normandy when Sweyn Forkbeard came blazing into Oxfordshire.

As king, the childless Edward managed to promise the throne to William of Normandy, but also to the Anglo-Danish Harold Godwinson of Wessex. He had also previously made Edward Atheling his heir, Edward being the son of Edmund Ironside, who had been usurped by Sweyn Forkbeard after the Oxford pogrom. Edward the Atheling died in 1057, but his son Edgar Atheling had every reason to think that he could claim the throne when The Confessor died. Which he did, in 1066, without confessing to anyone who his final choice of heir was.

So, three heirs, and just one possible outcome – war.

4

THE NORMANS
1066–1154

The Norman era began with 1066 and all that – William defeated Harold Godwinson at the Battle of Hastings, and gripped England with all the cold-hearted ruthlessness of a trust fund manager sorting out his pension.

The political opposition in Oxfordshire came from Edgar Atheling, one of three possible heirs tantalised with the possibility of the English crown by Edward the Confessor. Edgar was an important symbol for the Conqueror, as he had been proclaimed king by the Saxon royal council, the Witan, after the Battle of Hastings. Descended from King Alfred the Great, Edgar was a potent symbol of Englishness in the face of the Viking-descended, Norman-French-speaking invaders. He had the country's leading nobles and churchmen behind him, including Stigand, the Archbishop of Canterbury.

However, when Anglo-Saxon resistance withered away, Stigand switched allegiance. He arranged to meet with William the Conqueror, submitting to him after the Normans crossed the Thames at Wallingford, where the usurping king stayed for the night. Stigand and the other members of the Witan who had raised Edgar's dynastic hopes now persuaded him to bow before the Conqueror.

Edgar Atheling was a politician through and through, and recognised a winning side when he saw one. He swore fealty to William at his London coronation, and was amongst the first wave of Anglo-nobility to take his place in the Norman court.

Quite what state Oxford was in during the early Norman period is debatable. It had been stormed in 1067, and between 1066 and 1086 it lost more than 50 per cent of its houses, much of its area being described as 'waste' in the 1086 Domesday Book, when 400 of its 1,000 houses were in such a poor state that they were not liable for William's property tax. This suggests destruction on a scale to equal anything seen in the cities stormed by the Normans in the 'Wasting of the North' that followed the Conquest; but its exact cause – deliberate trashing, redevelopment, evacuation or disaster – is undocumented.

Whatever the cause of this impoverishment, Oxford wasn't alone. There is evidence that many villages in Oxfordshire were abandoned, and the monks of Eynsham are reported to have fled from their abbey in fear of their lives.

A Norman, Remigius, was installed at Dorchester Abbey when its Saxon abbot Wulfwig died in 1067; but the Bishop of Lincoln mopped up the land that had formerly belonged to the abbey, including Banbury, Cropredy, Great Milton and Thame.

By the middle of 1067 the section of the island secured by the Normans didn't extend much further north than Oxford, with London, the South East, East Anglia and the southern counties as far as Dorset safely in the bag. But so confident was William in his position that he sailed back to Normandy, taking with him much booty and a boatload of loyal Englishmen, including Edgar Atheling. England was left in the hands of the king's brother, Bishop Odo of Bayeux.

SAXON COMEUPPANCE

Historically, the Saxons had it coming to them. Five hundred years earlier they had bagged the land from the Britons, and now it was the Normans doing the land-grabbing. In Oxfordshire and elsewhere, the secured territory was parcelled out to Norman generals and churchmen, with hardly any pre-Conquest Saxon land-owners holding on to their property after the transition. One of the exceptions was Turchil of Arden, who had extensive lands on the Oxfordshire–Warwickshire border and managed to retain Drayton. A more usual outcome is illustrated by the fate of a Saxon called Orgar, who had to hand over his land at Berrick Salome to the Norman Milo Crispin, and work as one of his sub-tenants.

Most of the county went to King William's relatives Robert D'Oilly, William FitzOsbern and Odo of Bayeux. D'Oilly became High Sheriff of Oxfordshire, taking the title from its previous owner, a Saxon called Edwin. He rebuilt Oxford, clearing slums and erecting a motte and bailey castle in 1071 – including the Church of St George, the tower of which is still standing. He also built the first bridge over the Thames at Grandpont, the ances-tor of Folly Bridge, which presumably brought an end to Oxford's original oxen ford.

FitzOsbern went on to become Earl of Hereford, Gloucester, Worcester and Oxfordshire, one of England's richest landowners and castle builders. During William's absences, FitzOsbern ruled as the king's steward in all but name. One of his many prizes was the manor of Albury; but he did not keep it for long. FitzOsbern died in battle in 1070, and his English estates passed to his son Robert de Breteuil, who rebelled against King William, unsuccessfully, and was deprived of his lands and titles.

Odo of Bayeux owned manors in Headington, Bampton, Wootton and elsewhere. Like FitzOsbern he over-reached himself, enjoying a dose of hubris in 1082 when his attempt to rally knights to the cause of supplanting the pope floundered, and William stripped him of all his lands. Some of the territory Odo had held in Oxfordshire was given to William's loyal companion Wadard, a Battle of Hastings veteran, and one of the named figures on the Bayeux Tapestry.

Many other men took smaller portions of the plunder too, including Ralph de Bagpuis, who built the settlement still known as Kingston Bagpuize. It is pronounced 'bag-pews' rather than the very tempting 'bagpuss' (and was renamed Bagpipes in the Second World War by USAF airmen stationed here). The parish's full title is Kingston Bagpuize with Southmoor, the two villages being one. Southmoor has the dubious honour of having been owned by absentee landlords for more than a thousand years – Abingdon Abbey originally, then Bagpuis and his heirs, and currently St John's College, Oxford.

DOOM AND GLOOM, 1086

The stage was set for the most famous innovation of William's reign – the Domesday Book of 1086. It was given this title as its findings were intended to establish the basic economy of the country from then until Doomsday. It was basically an account book of monstrous proportions, detailing how much land each landowner had, and what that land was worth in terms of output.

The various royal estates of Oxfordshire netted the king £418 per annum, which is roughly £2 million in today's money. In addition, he received annual sums of £10 for a hawk and £23 for hounds (about £8,000 and £17,000 today), for hunting purposes. There was plenty of land for him to hunt in – the forests at Woodstock, Shotover, Stowood, Cornbury and Wychwood covered around 51,000 acres.

Oxfordshire was still a land divided by rivers. There were very few Thames crossings when the Normans arrived, which had always hindered trade and easy movement. Streatley and Wallingford had fords, and there were ferries at Bablockhythe, Caversham, Dorchester, Sandford and Swinford. But it was not until the turn of the twelfth century that bridges appeared at some of these sites, including at Oxford, on the site of the ford that had given the city its name. There was no Thames bridge on the stretch between Oxford and Wallingford until the fifteenth century.

At the time of the 1086 survey, only Oxford and Bampton had markets – all other settlements in Oxfordshire were small communities of self-sufficient tenant and sub-tenant smallholders.

EARLY GAMES OF MONOPOLY

After its original poor showing in 1086 as a town full of decrepit houses, Oxford rose in the following century to become a thriving market town, one of the biggest in the country. A guild merchant was established early on, a closed-shop institution which held the monopoly on the making and selling of goods. By the mid-twelfth century the by-invite-only guild merchant had become the most influential force in the city, and in this power and pride we can perhaps see the roots of the later riots which regularly shook the city, with the townsmen warring against the upstart students at the Johnny-come-lately university.

In 1155 Oxford's guild merchant was given the right to trade anywhere in England and Normandy, without having to pay tolls – the equivalent back then of being allowed into the EU trading bloc. This put Oxford's guild on a par with London and Winchester in terms of privileges, and the Oxford ox soon got very fat on the rich pickings. The rules jealously protected trades such as weaving and leather-working, stating that no non-guild member (and there were separate sub-guilds for each of the trades) was neither allowed to make goods within a wide radius of the city, nor to own a shop in the area.

The food markets, on the other hand, were a free-for-all in which traders were allowed to sell their wares – after paying a toll, of course. Oxford streets became signposts for what was sold in each location, with Cornmarket, Fish Street (St Aldate's), Horsemonger Street (Broad Street), Butcher Row (Queen Street) and the Butter Bench (at Carfax) all springing up in the twelfth century.

In 1199 King John granted the guild merchant and citizens of Oxford effective control of the city, for an annual payment of £63 and 5d (somewhere in the region of £45,000 in today's money). This was to be paid to the king directly, not through the usual middleman sheriff. This required the election of two bailiffs, to gather the money from the guild members, and a chief officer (later called mayor) to generally oversee things. A Guild Hall was built on the St Aldate's site, occupied in later years by the city's various town halls.

The earliest holder of this latter post was one Lawrence Kepeharme, who was out there intimidating the tax payers in 1204. He oversaw a weekly court dealing with offences and other matters affecting the guild. Kepeharm owned land in the St Aldate's area, and there was a hall and a street named after him. The name appears to be unique to this one Oxford family. The proto-mayor died in 1209, and Philip the Miller took over the job, only to be forced from office in 1216 after being found guilty of hanging some students, and therefore being largely responsible for one of the earliest '[Town and Gown' riots in the city.

One of the other major markets of the era, at Thame, received its charter around 1183. It had grown on 50 acres of land donated by the Bishop of Lincoln, divided into a series of acre and half-acre plots for rent-paying tenants who, in coughing up, freed themselves from the usual back-breaking and larder-emptying feudal dues to the lord of the manor. In 1219 the main road was diverted through Thame, and it has been a thriving market town ever since.

The bishop did similar things with his lands at Banbury, with about 1,300 residents living there in the early thirteenth century. It was already the second largest town in Oxfordshire, after Oxford.

Abingdon, Adderbury, Bampton, Banbury, Bicester, Burford, Chipping Norton, Eynsham, Henley, Middleton Stoney, Standlake, Witney and Woodstock all became locally important market towns in the early Norman period too. Burford already had its own guild merchant by the turn of the twelfth century. As the lord of the manor was an absentee, and as his bailiffs seem to have been particularly ineffective or lazy, the guild wielded some of his powers, and even used its own seal in the later thirteenth century like a miniature city state.

Burford's guild gradually took control of tolls, market organisation, bye-laws and the local court, all of which would normally have fallen to the agents of the lord of the manor. It even opened an annex at the parish church where a priest taught local children for free. This unorthodox system continued into the early seventeenth century, when a legal challenge finally put the guild in its place, and the progressive system disappeared in favour of traditional manorial control.

The old Guild Hall still stands, as a symbol of the once mighty Burford guild merchant. Similar buildings also survive in Abingdon and Chipping Norton.

View of the Market Place, Woodstock, from 1777.

LANDLORDS: ABSENT WITH LEAVE

Burford's lazy lord was not alone – the major local land-owners tended to be absentees from their Oxfordshire lands, and much of it was run by their bailiffs and shire-reeves (i.e. sheriffs), split into manors. Each manor had different types of land for crops, animals, meadows, woodland and fish ponds, and a mill (usually water-powered) for grinding corn. It was at this point in history that strip farming began, each strip 1 acre in size, which was the area that could be ploughed by a man and a team of oxen in one day – albeit a very strong man over the course of a very long working day. Tenants' strips of land were scattered across the manor, to make things equitable in terms of good land and not-so-good land.

Around half the week was spent working for the landowner. At busy times of year such as ploughing, haymaking and harvest time, the tenants were little more than slaves. The lords of the manor usually compensated them by holding a feast, or giving them meat, cheese or other foodstuffs in return.

In addition to all this free labour, the lord of the manor claimed rent for the land, and was able to raise or introduce other taxes as he saw fit. This was the nature of the feudal system, and it lasted until the Black Death caused social collapse in the mid-fourteenth century.

OXFORDSHIRE'S FIRST ZOO

Henry I (1100–1135) was William the Conqueror's son, gaining the throne after the death of his brother William II, nicknamed Rufus on account of his red beard. Henry was present when William was killed by an arrow during a hunting trip in the New Forest in Hampshire, and some historical conspiracy theorists have suggested that he was the mastermind of a plot to kill the king and snatch the throne. The jury is still out, and has no intention of returning.

Henry I earned the nickname Beauclerc – the Good Scholar – through his patronage of Oxford. There was no official university here yet, but reading between the lines (always a dangerous source of evidence), we can assume that it was already a place renowned for its schools. Henry founded Beaumont Palace in the city, at a site marked by modern Beaumont Street.

Henry and his queen, Matilda of Scotland, had other bases in Oxfordshire too, including Sutton Courtenay and Woodstock. He rebuilt the Royal Palace here, erecting a 7-mile-long stretch of wall around the park and installing wild animals. History records lions, lynx, camels and porcupines. These two sites – Oxford and Woodstock – were to be the homes and playgrounds of many monarchs to come.

Henry I's son Henry II (1133–1189) enlarged the estate, founding a settlement called New Woodstock nearby, to give his staff and retainers lodgings closer to the palace. There were over 500 people living there by the end of his reign.

DON'T STOP, FIEF!

Not many Norman-era buildings survive in Oxfordshire, but honourable mention should be made of the churches at Iffley and St Ebbes in Oxford. They

Norman doorway at St Ebbe's church, Oxford. (Photo by Jan Sullivan)

feature striking 'beaked heads' designs, and the example at St Ebbes is all the more remarkable for being the only remnant of the old church, set in the wall of a nineteenth-century rebuild. Iffley's Church of St Mary the Virgin, however, is a genuine Norman survival, built around 1160 by the St Remy family as a parish church for the houses on their manor estate.

Bloxham has one of the most impressive parish churches in England. It was founded around the same time as Iffley church, although most of the surviving parts are fourteenth century. At 60m tall, its tower is the highest in Oxfordshire. Almost as impressive is the early-twelfth-century church – another one dedicated to Mary – at Adderbury. Both these buildings are indicative of the relative wealth of this part of Oxfordshire in the Norman period.

Bloxham is one of the few places in the country where the Norman institution of feoffes survives. The name refers to a person in possession of land or rights called a 'fief'. In practice, the Bloxham feoffes consisted of between eight and sixteen local landowners responsible for certain aspects of village life and upkeep. They provided relief for the poor and repaired buildings and bridges, amongst other things, for which they were paid by the Crown. This local do-gooding continued until the First World War, and even today the Bloxham feoffes fulfil a charitable role in the village.

THE FIRST ANARCHY IN THE UK

Henry I's only legitimate son, William Adelin, had died in a shipwreck in 1120, along with one of Henry's several illegitimate children, Richard. This left his daughter Matilda as the only direct heir. She had been born on 7 February 1102 at Sutton Courtenay, and her parents could hardly have suspected the adventure that lay in store for her.

Etienne de Blois, the villain of the piece, was Henry's nephew. He disputed Matilda's claim and seized the throne after the death of the king in 1135, reigning as King Stephen, and leading to a period of civil war and lawless brutality known as the Anarchy.

Poor Oxford, just establishing itself as a European seat of learning, found itself at the heart of this dispute. It was the political base of Matilda, the rightful ruler. But she was not everyone's first choice in the succession. The fact that she was a woman did not go down well with patriarchal Norman aristocracy, and she was also a member of the hated Angevin dynasty.

Matilda had originally been the wife of Holy Roman Emperor Henry V (marrying him when she was just 8 years old), but after Henry died in 1125 she went on to become the wife of Geoffrey of Anjou, an 'Angevin'. Anjou was an enemy of the Duchy of Normandy, having recently tried to conquer it (the Kings of England also being the Dukes of Normandy, and therefore subservient to the King of France and at loggerheads with various rivals in the French homelands). As a direct consequence of this political game of Twister, Matilda had spent hardly any time in England prior to Henry's death, and that did not enamour her to the Anglo-Normans either.

Stephen had match-winning support in his claim from several religious and political ringleaders, including the Archbishop of Canterbury and Pope Innocent II, along with the all-important city of London. He was crowned king there, but over the following weeks he failed to win over many of the country's most powerful nobles, and he alienated many more, including his brother Bishop Theobald. Many of them sided with Matilda who, encouraged by the way the wind seemed to be blowing, set sail from France to England in 1139 to stake her claim to the island, while her husband Geoffrey of Anjou attacked Stephen's lands in Normandy.

After a few battles, Matilda made her way to London where she was crowned Queen Matilda; but the townsfolk rose up against her, and she retreated to Oxford, holing up at the castle.

Stephen besieged the city, and all looked lost for Matilda. But, in an escape bid similar to and every bit as daring as that of the imprisoned Mr Toad in Oxonian Kenneth Grahame's *The Wind in the Willows*, she donned a disguise and managed to slip out of the castle one freezing winter's night. Wearing white to blend in with the snowy landscape, she crossed the frozen Thames and escaped to the stronghold of Wallingford Castle.

Forces regrouped, and with her son Henry 'Curtmantle' (named after his fashion-setting short robes), Matilda eventually controlled the south-west of England, while Stephen controlled much of the south-east. But there were no more decisive battles, and the true horrors of the Anarchy now descended, a period possibly matched but not exceeded by the very grimmest events in this island's history. The Anglo-Saxon Chronicle famously comments that Stephen's nineteen-year reign was a time when

'Christ and his Saints slept'. After detailing the various tortures and hardships carried out by the lawless chieftains of the time, the chronicler – the last to write in the old Anglo-Saxon language – concluded:

> I know not how to, nor am I able to tell of, all the atrocities nor all the cruelties which they wrought upon the unhappy people of this country. It lasted throughout the nineteen years that Stephen was king, and always grew worse and worse. Never did a country endure greater misery, and never did the heathen act more vilely than they did.

In 1147 Matilda's main ally Robert of Gloucester died, and her hopes of victory died with him. She returned to Anjou, to which her husband Geoffrey had by now added the Dukedom of Normandy. In 1153 she and Henry were ready to reinvade England with a host of more than 3,000, and after much political wrangling and arm-twisting, Stephen was eventually forced to sign a truce.

The agreement they came to bypassed Stephen's own son Eustace in the succession in favour of Matilda's son, soon to become Henry II, first of the Plantagenet kings. In return, Stephen was allowed to remain on the throne, but he now had little power beyond the walls of his court. He died in 1154, and Henry II ascended with his wife Eleanor of Aquitaine. Matilda was still around to dream that the new empire – encompassing England, the east of Ireland and much of western France – would last forever.

By 1214, with the loss of Anjou and Normandy, this dream was in tatters and the Hundred Years' War that followed proved that the destructive spirit of the Anarchy was still flourishing.

5

THE PLANTAGENETS
1154–1485

Henry I built Beaumont Palace in Oxford in the 1130s, just beyond the city's North Gate. By palace standards it was small, but it remained a popular residence for royalty for 200 years, and parliaments were regularly held there.

The first record of Henry I using the building is Easter 1133. Henry II spent many Christmases there, and kings Richard I and John were both born at Beaumont. Edward I was the last monarch to use it. In 1275 he gave it to an Italian lawyer called Francesco Accorsi, as a gift for the diplomatic missions the man had undertaken for the English Crown.

One of the architects of Beaumont and other early stone buildings in Oxford was a mason called Elyas. His name appears – with such titles as 'Stonemason' and 'Engineer' – in various city accounts, and he would have been one of the most prominent and successful non-aristocrats of his age. He is first mentioned in 1187 as receiving money for work on the palace – renovation or extension, presumably – and by the next year Elyas was being paid daily for its upkeep, in addition to his other building fees.

Elyas the mason remained keeper of Beaumont until 1200, by which time he had become a rich man, working for kings Richard I and John at locations as diverse as Hastings, Rochester, the New Forest, the Tower of London, and again at Oxford, where he worked on the castle.

THE RISE OF ACADEMIC OXFORD

The religious institution founded by St Frideswide in the eighth century received a new lease of life in 1129 with the founding of St Frideswide's Priory. This was a magnet for scholars, and over the next 100 years, with the foundation of Osney Abbey and Rewley Abbey, followed by the Black, White and Grey Friars, Oxford became a centre of learning.

Teaching was already taking place in the early twelfth century, at a time when England had at last found a little breathing space after centuries of warfare. A man called Theobald d'Etamps was the first to title himself Master of Oxford, and in 1117 he was recorded as having sixty students. Another teacher had the name and title Walter Archdeacon of Oxford and Provost of the College of Secular Canons of St George in the Castle.

One of Walter's canons was Geoffrey of Monmouth, a Welsh scholar with a love of history and a vivid imagination to match. It was Geoffrey who claimed, amongst many other wildly wonderful things, that Oxford had been founded with the name Caer Memphric around 1000 BC by an evil British king called Mempricius, who was later eaten by wolves. Geoffrey recorded his pseudo-history in *The History of the Kings of Britain*, which first hit the shops in 1136. Historians have poured scorn on his revelations ever since, but it's still a highly entertaining romp.

King Henry II was the first Plantagenet monarch. He kick-started the embryonic university at Oxford by granting the city a royal charter that, through privileges and incentives, encouraged rudimentary economic and academic development. Chronicles mention Master Robert Puleyn as lecturer in divinity in 1133, and he was clearly part of what was by then an established centre of learning.

Early in the thirteenth century the office of Chancellor of the University was established. The first named holder of the post was Robert Grosseteste in 1224, the man credited with founding the tradition of scientific thought in Oxford. He had been Master of the School of Oxford since 1208, in an earlier version of the chancellor role. His main task was to keep an eye on general behaviour and standards, on behalf of the Bishop of Lincoln in whose diocese the university was. In Grossteste's day the university's only source of income was 52s (worth about £2,000 today), an annual fine from the townsmen as penance for the hanging of some students during the 1209 Town versus Gown riot.

Scholar-friars settled in Oxford in large numbers, drawn by the city's academic reputation. The Dominicans, or Black Friars, came first, in 1221. They were soon followed by the Franciscans – the Grey Friars – in 1224. The game was properly afoot in 1229, when the temporary closure of the University of Paris caused many more students and teachers to move to Oxford. The Grey Friars expanded their *studium* on land behind St Ebbe's church, and it became the largest Franciscan house outside London. It was here that leading theologian, philosopher and prime mover of the early university, John Duns Scotus (1266–1308), received his formative education.

The earliest university-affiliated residences were the halls, which were simply lodging houses not dissimilar to modern halls of residence. The college concept, in which every student accesses university education via a college, was founded by Walter de Merton, Chancellor of England. This collegiate system began with Walter's foundation of Merton College in 1265, as a community of students bound together by residence, rules, traditions, chapel, refectory and, a little later, the 'quad' layout of rooms overlooking a central decorative outdoor space.

The linking of a college with a particular source of students was established in the reign of Richard II by William of Wykeham, founder of New College in 1379. His college was to be fed by pupils from Winchester School. Since then, colleges have often been associated with particular schools, towns, or whole regions.

The booming university entailed lots of new building, which required good building material. The quarries at Wheatley, Headington, Burford and Taynton did very well in supplying the demand over the next few hundred years. The university phenomenon also fed other trades such as bookbinding, parchment making and paper making, culminating in the establishment of the University Press in 1583.

The first building actually planned, financed and built by the joint heads of the university itself was the Divinity School, begun in the 1450s. The chief mason involved was Richard Winchcombe, a New College employee who also worked on Adderbury church's chancel in 1408, and on the fan-vaulted Wilcote Chapel in North Leigh church. The Wilcote Chapel had been commissioned by Lady Elizabeth Blackett in memory of her first husband Sir John Wilcote, in 1440, the last year in which Winchcombe was active.

The Divinity School included the university's first proper book collection – Duke Humphrey's Library, named after Humphrey of Lancaster, Duke of Gloucester, brother of Henry V. He had died in 1447, donating 281 manuscripts to the university (only three of which have survived).

The university was exempt from many of the laws that applied to laymen, and from the early days was able to establish its own rules. This fed the famous 'Town versus Gown' divide in Oxford. The apartheid lasted into the nineteenth century, with annual head-to-heads.

Students were originally clerics, with tonsures (the shaven heads associated with monks), and for serious legal matters they answered to religious courts – and, ultimately, the Papacy. The rise of the hall and, later, college system was an attempt to maintain the clerical/secular divide. Students had originally lodged with townsfolk as 'chamberdekyns', and had succumbed to the distinctly secular habits (i.e. wine, women and song) of the ordinary citizen. Herded into halls under a master or principal, the intention was that they would avoid the many temptations of the flesh to be found on the streets of Oxford.

By the early part of the thirteenth century there were around 1,500 students living in Oxford, making up about one third of the population. Rents rocketed, and a rent board had to be established to quell the inflation. Everyone took advantage, with food prices soaring too, all of which fuelled the resentment of the less well-off residents who belonged to neither guild nor university. The tension constantly bubbled over into brawling.

WAR OF THE ROSE

Godstow Abbey was founded as a nunnery in 1133 by Edith, widow of Sir William Launceline. The site is most famous for its associations with Rosamund Clifford, mistress of Henry II, and it was Henry's financial favours that kept the foundation running in its early years. Poignant ruins of the abbey still stand at Godstow, near Oxford.

When 'Fair Rosamund' died in 1176, it was rumoured that she had been killed by Henry's jealous queen, Eleanor. The lovers' favourite meeting place had been in the Hunting Lodge at Woodstock Palace. In legend this lodge lay at the centre of a labyrinth, which Eleanor navigated by following a trail of thread before giving Rosamund the choice of stabbing or poisoning herself. She chose the poison.

Woodstock Palace shortly before demolition, 1711.

In reality, Rosamund had been educated at the nunnery as a girl, and when the affair with Henry ended in 1174, she retired here, dying two years later at the age of 30, cause unknown. She was buried in the abbey church beside the altar, and her tomb became a shrine. In 1191, two years after Henry's death, Bishop Hugh of Lincoln paid a visit to Godstow and didn't look kindly on the growing cult of Rosamund. He ordered the tomb to be relocated to the churchyard.

Rosamund's tomb allegedly had a dark-humoured rhyming couplet inscribed on its lid:

> *Hic jacet in tumba Rosamundi non Rosamunda,*
> *Non redolet sed olet, quae redolere solet.*

which translates as:

> Here lies in the tomb the rose of the world, not a pure rose:
> She who used to smell sweet still smells, but not sweetly.

However, when the remnants of the tomb were examined in 1631 the only inscription to be found read simply, 'TUMBA ROSAMUNDAE'.

OSNEY ABBEY AND THE CHATTERING CLASSES

Edith Frome, wife of High Sheriff of Oxfordshire Robert d'Oilly's son Robert D'Oyly the Younger, founded Osney Abbey in Oxford after an encounter with magpies in 1129. She was walking by the Thames, when, according to an account by 1660s chronicler Anthony Wood, she saw 'a great company of pyes gathered together on a tree, making a hideous noise with their chattering'. They were there on the following day, and the next, 'seeming as 'twere to direct their chatterings to her'.

Edith consulted Radulphus, a monk of Oxford's St Frideswide's Abbey, for advice. After witnessing the magpies, he declared: 'these are no pyes, but so many poor souls in purgatory that do begg and make all this complaint for succour and relief'. Edith founded the abbey, and Radulphus, whom Wood terms 'the wiliest pye of them all', became its first prior, and Edith an abbess.

In reality, Edith founded the abbey as penance for her years as the mistress of King Henry I.

Osney Abbey ruins in 1641.

The abbey, on the banks of the Thames in the part of Oxford now known as Osney Island, grew to be one of the most influential in the country. It provided leaders for other religious foundations, and attracted men of learning – all grist for the embryonic university mill. In 1199 it was granted the church of St George's at Oxford Castle.

In April 1222 a church council met at Osney Abbey, with a mission to apply a new set of Catholic rules in England, known as the Lateran decrees. In 1238 Cardinal Odo, the papal legate, made a visit to Oxford's chancellor Robert Grosseteste, to make sure the Catholic law was flourishing. Grossteste was a world-renowned academic, devout church man, and friend of Pope Gregory IX. Under his guidance the university had moved from a stop-start, largely improvised academic free-for-all, to a well organised place of study finally able to rival Europe's great seat of learning, Paris.

Osney Abbey was the venue for Odo's visit, and in the evening a delegation of students arrived at the abbey's Guests' Hall requesting audience with the legate to show their respects. They took grave offence at being turned away by one of the cardinal's guards, and forced their way indoors. The guards reacted by drawing their swords, but the students disarmed them and beat them with fists and staves.

Things got out of hand when Cardinal Odo's brother, who was overseeing the cooking due to his sibling's morbid fear of poisoning, threw scalding broth into the face of a chaplain. One of the students cried out: 'Fie for shame, shall we suffer this?', and shot the guest chef with an arrow. Cardinal Odo was locked in the abbey church tower for safety during the ensuing riot, while a plea for help was sent to King Henry III, residing with his court at Abingdon Abbey.

An armed guard arrived a few hours later to escort Odo to the king. Oxford University was effectively shut down once again, and grovelling letters of apology were sent to the pope. The future of the institution looked uncertain, and many scholars were forced to complete their studies at Salisbury, Northampton or Paris. Some of the ringleaders of the riot were hunted down and arrested, and some executed. Osney Abbey survived the ordeal, but its pre-eminence in the country was over.

Henry III did not hold a grudge against the abbey, as far as we can tell, and it is recorded that the 15-year-old spent Christmas at Osney Abbey in 1222 'with great revelling mirth'.

HENRY III GETS IN THE PROVISIONS

Henry III (1207–72) spent much of his reign in Oxford's Beaumont Palace and Woodstock Palace. According to a historian writing in 1869: 'In 1238 he narrowly escaped assassination there [Woodstock] by a Priest named Ribbaud. This man, who was either insane, or feigned to be so, climbed through a window at night to the Chamber of the King and Queen. He was discovered while entering by a devout woman, Margaret Byet, and taken to Oxford, and torn to pieces by Horses.'

Woodstock Palace was a major drain on Henry's resources. During his reign he spent £3,300 on repairs and improvements – about £2.5 million in today's money.

Civil war stalked England throughout the medieval period. In 1215, when Oxford-born King John refused to abide by the Magna Carta, which had been drawn up in that year, several barons sided with Louis VIII, the king of France, and went to war against the English king. This isn't as disloyal as it might sound, as in those days the aristocracy was culturally, and linguistically, very French, and English monarchs owned large chunks of France. The main impact of this conflict in Oxfordshire was the refortification of the castle at Oxford, with the local church of St Budoc's knocked down to provide the heavy masonry. At the same time a deep town ditch was dug, with a stone wall on the outside. Parts of this wall have survived in the gardens at New College and in the vicinity.

John died of dysentery in 1216, and the war petered out in 1217, but discontent was not far below the surface. The Provisions of Oxford were drawn up in 1258 in Oxford, following another Barons' War. The situation calmed down temporarily and the opposing sides called a truce, meeting in Oxford for what has since been dubbed the first English parliament. Spearheaded by the Earl of Leicester, Simon de Montfort, and eleven likeminded barons, along with twelve men chosen by Henry III, the Provisions of Oxford declaration built on the Magna Carta, putting the barons' rights on a firm legal footing. The new deal established a fifteen-strong Privy Council, monitored by a parliament which was to meet three times a year.

The Provisions of Oxford were distributed to the country's sheriffs in three languages – Latin, French and English, marking the first time official documents had used the native tongue since the last entries of the Anglo-Saxon Chronicle in the reign of King Stephen.

The Provisions of Oxford were overturned by Henry, backed by the pope, in 1261. The result was the Second Barons' War in 1263, which dragged on for five years.

Many students who had been forced to leave Oxford after the riot and murder at Osney Abbey joined Simon de Montfort's rebellion, marching under their own Oxford Scholars' banner at the Battle of Northampton in 1264. The sword was mightier than the pen on that particular day, though, and the king's men won.

Simon de Montfort was killed at the Battle of Evesham in August 1265. His head was displayed for several months afterwards on London Bridge.

EDWARD ONE

On 18 July 1290 King Edward I (1139–1207) expelled all Jews from England. Many had left Oxford already, and in 1290 only ten Jewish property holders remained. Their property was confiscated, and the street that had been called The Great Jewry for the last 250 years became Fish Street. Tradition maintains that some Jews converted to Christianity in order to stay in Oxford, and produced bibles in Hebrew and Latin.

In 1295 Oxford sent representatives to Edward I's national parliament, meeting for the first time, in a form that had been largely shaped by the doomed Simon de Montfort thirty years earlier. The gathering soon became known as the Commons – not because the members were commoners (they were all French-speaking aristocrats), but from the French word *commune*, implying community representatives.

One of Oxfordshire's leading members of Parliament was Andrew de Pyrie, who attended thirteen sittings between 1295 and 1313, far more than most other proto-MPs of the time. Sir John Harcourt went to parliament in 1322, the first of many from that family to represent Oxfordshire through the decades; and Thomas Chaucer, descendant of the writer Geoffrey Chaucer, was Speaker of the Commons from 1407 to 1415.

EDWARD TWO

Contemporary critics held Edward II's love of 'peasant pursuits' against him – he appears to have been the first monarch to have possessed that rarest of royal gifts, 'the common touch'. Throughout his life (1284–1337) he enjoyed gardening, thatching roofs, talking with the staff at Beaumont, and that most Oxfordian of pursuits, rowing. These days such a skill is PR golddust, but back then it was taken as yet another sign of mental weakness. He was certainly unpopular with many of the country's powerful noblemen and clergy, leading to yet another period of civil war.

The most surprising plot to dethrone Edward came from an Oxford University student called John Deydras. Oxford was one of the places where Edward was actually popular, as he had given money to Oxonian Adam de Brome to found Oriel College (originally named The Hall of the Blessed Mary at Oxford), the first university institution to receive royal patronage.

John Deydras (aka John of Powderham, after the village of that name in Devon) announced in 1318 that he was the rightful heir to the throne, and issued a proclamation to this effect. He then visited Oxford's royal seat, Beaumont Palace, hoping to take up residence.

The pretender was reported to look like Edward, but with one very distinctive feature – he only had one ear.

Deydras claimed that as a royal toddler he had been playing in the courtyard at Beaumont, when a hungry sow attacked him and bit off his ear. The royal nurse, fearing for her life, took the boy to a carter's house and swapped him for the carter's own son, who was the same age as her charge.

John Deydras, the 'real' Edward, proposed that the imposter king's love of rural pursuits, bisexual tastes and lack of military skills were all clues to the fact that he was not the divinely appointed monarch. To put things right, he offered to face the king in single combat.

On this occasion John Deydras was simply kicked off the premises, but later in the year he was arrested and brought before the real Edward II. The king greeted him with the words 'Welcome, my brother!' and, according to legend, offered him a job as court jester. But Edward's queen Isabella failed to see the joke, and in the end Deydras, refusing to change his changeling story, was imprisoned in Oxford's Bocardo prison, charged with sedition.

John Deydras admitted that he had made up the whole story, but did himself no favours when he declared that while walking across Christ Church Meadow, his pet cat had spoken to him, revealing itself as the Devil, and suggesting the pretender ruse. Both Deydras and his poor cat were hanged, and the man's body was burnt afterwards.

On 9 June 1312 a weary party stopped at an inn in Deddington, several days into their trek south from Scarborough Castle. In their midst was Piers Gaveston, favourite of King Edward II, a hate figure for a large group of rebellious earls. Gaveston's personal gaoler, the Earl of Pembroke, had promised to let him live – as long as he forfeited the lands Edward had given him.

Christ Church Meadow, where Dreydas and his cat plotted together.

But when Pembroke took the opportunity to visit his wife at nearby Bampton, Gaveston's enemies surrounded the inn. His apathetic guards refused to defend him and he was forced to surrender to the Earl of Warwick, his bitterest enemy. Ten days after his stay in Deddington, after being chained and imprisoned, Gaveston was stabbed to death and beheaded at Blacklow Hill in Warwickshire. Deddington's coat of arms shows a black eagle in chains, a reference to poor Piers and the judgement of his peers.

EDWARD THREE... AND ALMOST FOUR

A portrait of Edward of Woodstock, more famously known as the Black Prince (1330–76), hangs in the hall at Christ Church in Oxford. Edward was the eldest son of King Edward III (1312–77) and was the embodiment of the patriotic English knight, and first Knight of the Garter in 1348. He was born in Woodstock and had his main residence at Wallingford. His early death from dysentery denied him the throne; and his several illegitimate children and reputation for brutality somewhat undermined his image as the flower of chivalry.

The Christ Church portrait was painted in the eighteenth century, and was known to be based not on images of the Black Prince himself, but on a handsome Oxford butcher's son.

BACON FRIAR

Franciscan friar and philosopher Roger Bacon (*c.*1219–*c.*1292) was the preeminent thinker of his age, nicknamed Doctor Mirabilis, or Doctor of Miracles. He was a master at Oxford, teaching Aristotelian philosophy, amongst other things, and renowned as an alchemist and magician, which can be interpreted as meaning that he was way ahead of his time, and his science looked like sorcery to the less gifted brains of the time.

According to one probably apocryphal story, Bacon once dressed himself as a common thatcher to meet a deputation from Cambridge University. The students from the 'Other Place' were so dismayed to find such a formidable intellect amongst the common populace that they ran back home, afraid of being put to shame by Oxford's genuine academics.

Amongst the man's many words of wisdom were 'Half of science is about asking the right questions' and the famous 'A little learning is a dangerous thing, but none at all is fatal'.

Bacon lived in a Gothic structure that once decorated the southern end of Folly Bridge. It was said to have been so cunningly constructed that it would collapse on anyone who thought themselves cleverer than Bacon. It was built a century before Bacon's time; and it did indeed come tumbling down in the end, demolished in 1779 during road-widening and sold by auction. It was called Friar Bacon's Study, and the nearby bridge was called Friar's Bridge. It was only in 1611 that the name 'Folly' was applied to both, when Thomas Waltham, aka Mr Welcome, made an ill-advised extra storey extension to Bacon's old study. Locals renamed it Welcome's Folly.

THE LOLLARD BRAND

John Wycliffe spent his academic career at Oxford, graduating from Merton and then becoming a master at Balliol. He also lodged in buildings at Queen's College. From here he wrote books and treatises which formed the basis of Protestantism, and miraculously enough he managed to survive the ire of the Church, even when he had reached the conclusion that the pope was the Antichrist.

Wycliffe is most famous for translating the Bible into English in 1384, which was viewed as heretical at the time. His followers, the Lollards, were thorns in the side of the Church for decades to come.

The 'Constitutions of Oxford' church police session of 1410, headed by Oriel College alumnus Thomas Arundel, Archbishop of Canterbury, attempted to stamp out all this heresy. The judges picked out 247 propositions from the work of John Wycliffe as being particularly dangerous, banning much of his writing, and adding that translating any part of the Bible into English was heresy, punishable by death. Lincoln College, founded in 1427, was specifically set up to oppose Lollardism and Wycliffites, which is a very impressive measure of the man's impact.

It had its work cut out, as Oxfordshire remained a hotbed of Lollardism for at least another 100 years. A self-educated weaver called James Wyllys was arrested at Henley in 1462 for being a Lollard, and was burnt to death. Records also mention unrepentant Lollards at Chinnor and Thame in 1464.

The desire to have an English version of the Bible persisted, and in the reign of Henry VIII there were still people being dubbed 'Lollards' in Burford, Witney, Asthall, Henley and Standlake. If caught, the heretics were made to carry out some form of penance, and were branded on the cheek.

THE BLACK DEATH

The Black Death, ravaging the land in 1348–49, 1361–62 and 1369, is thought to have wiped out half of the Oxfordshire population. Much cleared land turned to scrub and then back to forest. Some villages had their populations reduced to single figures. On the manor at Tusmore, the open fields were converted into parkland, as there was simply no one left to work them. The 1,200 acres at Steeple Barton turned to scrub. Tilgarsley near Eynsham was abandoned, having had fifty-two tenant families in 1279, and not a single one by 1359. Witney Manor, which had expanded just a few decades earlier after forest clearance, noted in 1349 that there was no one willing to take on the land. In Cuxham near Watlington, all twelve of the village's tenant farmers died in the 1349 outbreak.

Many of Oxford University's halls stood empty after the plague, some of them losing all their students in the first outbreak. One such institution, Gloucester Hall, closed its doors forever in 1349 and only lingers as the basis of the name Gloucester Green, site of the modern bus station and market.

The most vivid illustration of these grimmest of times can be found in the comments of a jury of 1378, deciding whether to give the go-ahead for the development of 13 acres of real estate in north-east Oxford. The land had no buildings or enclosures of any kind, boasting only an all-purpose dump for sewage, rubbish and, when an outbreak caused a logjam of bodies, plague victim corpses. The only people to frequent the spot were criminals and prostitutes. Something had to be done, the jurors concurred, and gave planning permission to Chancellor of England (and Bishop of Winchester) William of Wykeham. On these unpromising foundations, New College was born. The 'plague mound' can still be seen in its grounds.

The county's markets stagnated as a result of the massive drop in population, with some trades being killed off altogether. The last Oxford weaver, of whom there had been sixty just fifty years earlier, died in 1323. This left lots of land vacant, most of which was scooped up by the university.

WOOLLY THINKING

In terms of clouds and silver linings, the Black Death was actually very good for Oxfordshire's surviving would-be tenants – known as villeins, origin of the modern word 'villain' – who suddenly found themselves in a sellers' market. Rather than working on the old terms of back-breaking work for the price of an annual dole of food, they could now command wages. Rents were reduced, and the days spent working for the lord of the manor were reduced to one a week. This meant the lords had to pay workers, lure in the increasingly mobile villeins, or expand the already thriving slave trade. There were lots of non-freemen – known as churls – desperate for the basics of a roof over their heads and the occasional meal. They tended to work for the tenants and sub-tenants.

The landscape changed radically as a result. Many strip fields disappeared, and Oxfordshire had its first extensive sheep herds. Sheep were non-labour-intensive livestock, and could be looked after by a single shepherd, with a dog to chase off wolves. Wool was already a very profitable product, and places like Witney began to thrive on the trade. Oxford was in on the act early too, with a Weavers' Guild, one of England's earliest, formed in 1130. This faded at the turn of the next century; but Witney flourished.

There had been a wool fulling mill in Witney as early as 969, and two more had appeared by the close of the thirteenth century. The manor of Witney was owned by the Bishop of Lincoln, who reaped most of his riches from keeping sheep, here and elsewhere. Witney blankets, made from Witney wool, became the defining product of Oxfordshire.

This sheep craze had a negative side for tenants in some areas, where expanding flocks resulted in evictions. But in general, the later fourteenth century saw the good times return to Oxfordshire – or arrive for the first time, depending on how you want to look at it. New markets gained licences, and new castles were built, including one at Banbury. Some of these were short-lived – at Bampton, Deddington, Middleton Stoney, Mixbury and Woodstock, for example.

STUDENT LIFE IS A RIOT

There had been many violent 'Town versus Gown' riots – i.e. Oxford townsfolk versus university students – prior to 1355, but that particular year saw the most extreme example. The conflict kicked off on St Scholastica's Day, 10 February.

In the Swindlestock Tavern at Carfax in Oxford a group of students including ringleaders Walter Spryngheuse and Roger de Chesterfield complained about the poor quality of the beer. The taverner John de Bereford, who was also Mayor of Oxford, swore at them, and the students began breaking bottles and fighting. In the time-honoured tradition, St Martin's church bell at Carfax was rung to summon the 'Town' and the bell on the university church of St Mary summoned the 'Gown'.

John de Bereford brought in 2,000 reinforcements from outside the city, and they advanced with the ominous chant, *'Slay, Slay! Havoc, havoc! Smite fast! Give good knocks!'* Some of the university's halls were ransacked, and over three days sixty-two students were killed. The mayor appealed to King Edward III to take the town's side in the dispute, but the king sided with the university. The mayor and his bailiffs were sentenced to carry out a penance: they had to attend a Mass for the souls of the sixty-two dead students, then and on every succeeding St Scholastica's Day. The top section of the church tower at Carfax was knocked down too, to prevent the Town from using it as a surrogate castle, as they had in the past.

The town was stripped of most of its power, with the university gaining control of the various weights and measures and laws formerly held by the Oxford guilds. Even more drastically, the Town had to swear a resurrected oath (first formulated after similar Town/Gown troubles in 1213) recognising the university's privileges and pre-eminence in the city. They had to reaffirm this each year, going on bended knee to the vice-chancellor of the university with sixty-two symbolic citizens and handing over sixty-two silver pennies.

Memory dies hard in Oxford, and this ritual humiliation and one-upmanship was only abolished in 1825. At the 600th anniversary of the St Scholastica's Day riot in 1955 hatchets were finally buried when the vice-chancellor gave an honorary degree to the Mayor of Oxford in the Sheldonian Theatre, and he in turn was made a freeman at the Town Hall.

The Swindlestock Tavern, which had opened in 1250, called last orders in 1709, by which time it had long been known as The Mermaid Tavern. The site, and the riot, are marked with a plaque at Carfax, low down on the wall of Marygold House, currently occupied by Santander Bank.

HENRY IV AND HENRY V
PARTS ONE AND TWO

According to John Davenport, writing in 1869:

> Henry the Fourth made Oxford and Woodstock his headquarters
> in the year 1400, at the period of the Conspiracy to restore Richard

the Second to the Throne. And the heads of the Duke of Surrey and
the Earl of Salisbury, cut off at Cirencester, were conveyed on long
poles to King Henry at Oxford ... Many Knights and Esquires were
beheaded in Oxford Castle at this eventful time.

Henry V, born 9 August 1388 and crowned 16 April
1413, was educated at Queen's College in Oxford from
the age of 11, and lived in rooms there. His tutor was his
uncle, Cardinal Beaufort. Part of an inscription preserved
in the north window of the library at Queen's describes
Henry (in translation from Latin) as: 'The Victor of His
foes, and of Himself.' This is a reference to Henry over-
coming his youthful hedonism to become a triumphant
monarch – the main theme of Shakespeare's three plays
Henry IV Parts One and Two, and *Henry V*.

Henry V is also associated with All Souls: the French
Wars that had culminated in the English victory at
Agincourt (1415) and the marriage of Henry V to
Katherine of France were uppermost in the founders'
minds when they made their dedication in 1438. The
college was founded not just as a place of learning but
as a chantry, a place of prayer endowed with money
to act as a permanent memorial to the dead. The High
Street gateway of the college, decorated with carved
souls, symbolises this. At the foundation, warden and
fellows were instructed to pray for the souls of all the
faithful departed, and in particular 'the illustrious
Prince Henry, late King of England, Thomas, Duke of
Clarence, and of all the Dukes, Earls, Barons, Knights,
Esquires, and others who fell in the war for the Crown
of France'.

(EDWARD) 4 + (RICHARD) 3 = (HENRY) 7

Edward IV (1442–83) favoured the palace at Langley over the one at Woodstock. Legend says that it was during a hunt in Wychwood Forest that he first met and instantly fell in love with his future queen, the widow Lady Elizabeth Grey, daughter of Sir Richard Woodville. The pair married in secret, and it was all very shocking at the time as Edward was already betrothed to Princess Bonne of Savoy. Marrying a subject, and a widowed one at that, was scandal indeed.

Edward and Elizabeth had ten children together (and he had several more through his various extra-marital affairs). These were all declared illegitimate in 1484, in order to clear the path to the throne for Richard III. The Act that achieved this was then repealed by Henry VII, and the children and their heirs were happily legitimate once again.

Edward and Elizabeth were benefactors of Oxford University. Records note that they stayed in rooms at the newly completed Magdalen College on 22 September 1481. They had entered the city by torchlight, and were welcomed by the University Chancellor Lionel Woodville, who was Elizabeth's brother.

Richard III (1452–85) paid a visit to Oxford early in his reign, and his chief lasting impact on the city was the passing of an act which gave the university the licence to export or import books as and when it desired. He held court at Magdalen College, where he heard disputations. He was treated to feasts there, and on one occasion thanked his hosts by presenting them with 'fat bucks from his Forest'.

Richard had many enemies, including John de Vere, the 13th Earl of Oxford. De Vere was one of the

Lancastrian commanders under Henry-soon-to-be-the-Seventh at the Battle of Bosworth in 1485. He was the mastermind behind a battlefield formation called, after him, 'the Oxford Wedge' – an arrow-shaped phalanx of men that penetrated Richard's main host at Bosworth and helped turn the battle. The 13th Earl of Oxford had played a key role in bringing to an end 331 years of Plantagenet rule.

One of the many men who prospered after the victory of Henry VII was William Cope. He became a member of the king's privy council and Cofferer of the Household, the man responsible for paying wages to the royal staff. He built Hanwell Castle on the proceeds, beginning the building in 1498. It was never intended as a castle in the defensive sense of the word, but was simply a house with battlements. It was the first large-scale brick building in north Oxfordshire.

Lord Francis Lovell – 'Lovell the Dog' to his enemies – had last been seen fleeing the Battle of Stoke in 1487, having supported the pretender Lambert Simnel in a Yorkist plot to remove the newly installed Lancastrian Henry VII. The Earl of Oxford was instrumental in Henry's victory, and Lovell probably fled due to a pre-battle agreement of 'no quarter'. This meant that there would be no mercy on the field, i.e. no survivors. Lovell and Simnell were the only survivors among the Yorkist rebel leaders.

Hanwell Castle.

The ruins of Minster Lovell Hall.

In 1708 Lovell was suposedly discovered in a secret room at Minster Lovell House near Burford, seated at a table with book, pen, paper and faithful dog. He had been there for 221 years, trapped after the faithful servant who locked him in inconveniently died. As the air now gushed into the deathly chamber, Lovell's and the dog's bones turned to dust.

The fact that Minster Lovell was owned by King Henry Tudor's uncle Jasper makes it a very unlikely hiding spot for an anti-Tudor, and a more credible story says that Lovell escaped to Scotland and eventually won a pardon.

6

THE TUDORS
1485–1603

Like so many monarchs before him, Henry VII was a frequent resident at Woodstock Palace where, to escape the headaches of rebuilding the shattered country, he was fond of staging court entertainments. One of these, a slapstick morality play called *The Necromancer*, was performed on Palm Sunday, 1501, soon after the marriage of his eldest son, Prince Arthur, to Katherine of Aragon.

Arthur was educated at Magdalen College in Oxford. He died at the age of 15, shortly after his wedding, but is said to have been a keen and able scholar. Magdalen College president Richard Mayhew had been one of the deputation sent to Spain to collect Katherine prior to the marriage.

Arthur paid a last visit to Oxford in 1501 on his way to join Katherine at Ludlow Castle. His reception at Magdalen was recorded by his hosts:

> He was lodged in the Apartments of the President; Rushes were provided for the Prince's bedchamber; he was treated with a brace of Pike and a brace of Tench; both his Highness and his Train received presents of Gloves, and were refreshed with red wine, claret, and sack.

Prince Arthur's premature death at the age of 15 denied the world a flesh-and-blood King Arthur – Henry had chosen the name specifically to tap into a pan-British sense of nationalism. Instead, England had to make do with the royal crumbs from the Round Table, in the shape of Arthur's younger brother Henry VIII.

Magdalen tower was completed in 1509, the year in which Henry VII died. Choristers from Magdalen College sang a Requiem Mass for him, Henry being a patron of the college. This Mass is still sung for Henry each year, along with another Tudor tradition – the May Morning hymn. Every 1 May crowds gather to hear choristers greet the dawn with a burst of song from the top of Magdalen College bell tower at 6 a.m.

HENRY VIII AND THE REFORMATION

In 1518, in the calm before the Reformation storm, Henry VIII and Queen Katherine – Arthur's widow, now married to Henry – fled London to escape a bout of the sweating sickness, setting up temporary court in Abingdon. There had been an outbreak ten years earlier, and there was to be another ten years later. This suggests a cycle of some kind, but no one knows for sure what this illness, sometimes called the English Sweat, was. It killed many, but not all, of its victims, and previous sufferers gained no immunity from fresh attacks. Even more peculiarly, it tended to afflict rich households and previously healthy young people. It was a virus associated with rich, active lifestyles – which is why it made sense for Henry and Katherine to seek the safety of Abingdon.

Oxfordshire's monasteries, abbeys, priories and friaries were all dissolved and confiscated in Henry's reign. The background to this includes a general disillusionment with the state of religion in England. In Oxfordshire, a 1517 commission had found many of the parish churches to be in poor condition. At Brightwell Baldwin, for example, the church chancel was falling down, and the glass from the windows was long gone. It was also claimed that church services were not being run properly, or not being run at all; and yet it is worth noting that it is the victors who write history, and the Anglican Church ushered in by Henry was never going to have anything positive to say about the Catholic Church it had replaced.

The Dissolution of the Monasteries was a drawn-out process, beginning in 1536 and with the final mopping up done in 1541, following the Act of Supremacy of 1534 by which Henry had broken with Rome to become head of his own Church of England. In addition to closing the monasteries, this also involved stripping ordinary churches of their Catholic trappings and riches. Much of the church treasure was not taken directly by Henry, but by self-serving churchwardens. In Thame, for example, the church silver was sold for over £300 – about £85,000 in today's money – and the ill-gotten gains went into the churchwardens' pockets.

In general, Oxfordshire's clergy did not oppose the revolution that had struck the Church. Most of them took the Oath of Supremacy; but there were exceptions. Sir Adrian Fortescue of Stonor Park flatly refused, and spoke out against the drastic reforms from the pulpit. He joined one of the rebellions against the new Church, and was executed for his defiance in 1539.

Abingdon Abbey, in the town where Henry had sought sanctuary in 1518, was surrendered willingly by its last abbot, Thomas Rowland, who had supported the Act of Royal Supremacy which ushered in the dissolution. The buildings were handed over in 1538, and in reward Rowland received the manor of Cumnor.

St Frideswide's Priory in Oxford, along with Littlemore Priory, had been dissolved early on. Henry's right-hand man, Cardinal Wolsey, had done the deed in April 1524, carrying out his plan to use Frideswide's buildings and income as the basis for his new foundation, Cardinal College. Like all Henry's right-hand men, the position proved temporary, and after Wolsey's fall from power in 1530, the king took over the premises and renamed it Henry the Eighth College in 1532. He paid his first visit to the college that year and was said to have been entertained with 'great solemnity'. The college was refounded yet again, this time as Christ Church, fourteen years later.

Dorchester Abbey was among the first of the dissolutions in 1536. Its Augustinian monks were scattered, and many of the buildings were repurposed. The huge church became the Abbey Church of St Peter and St Paul, a wonderfully out-of-scale parish church in the small village of Dorchester. Henry used the other abbey property to found another college, dedicated to the Holy Trinity, but this was closed down during the reign of his son Edward VI.

Bruern Abbey was closed in 1536 too. It was bought by Sir Anthony Cope of Hanwell, ancestor of the Cope baronets. The family built a baroque country house here in 1720 on the site of the abbey.

Osney Abbey was grabbed in 1539. The church was refounded as a cathedral, and its last abbot, Robert King, became the first Bishop of Oxford. The see was transferred to Christ Church Cathedral, the chapel of Christ Church College, in 1546, and Osney's bell, Great Tom, was moved to Christ Church too. After this, the Osney buildings were abandoned and slowly crumbled away. The church tower was standing in the 1640s, and there were still some ruins to rummage through in 1720 when Thomas Hearne of Oxford's St Edmund's Hall made some sketches of the site.

Rewley Abbey also fell prey to the land-grab in 1539. Its abbot, Nicholaus Austen, had offered Henry's henchman Thomas Cromwell £100 – about £45,000 in today's money – to save the abbey three years earlier, suggesting that it could be converted into a college like St Frideswide's. Cromwell didn't take the bait, and the site was levelled, with some of the stone used to strengthen the tower at St Mary Magdalen's church in Oxford. The only bit that survives is a stone gateway, by the Oxford canal.

Godstow Abbey was seized in 1539, and bought by George Owen, who converted it into Godstow House. Its last abbess was given a pension of £50 a year (about

Rewley Abbey remains, as they appeared in 1823.

£21,000 in today's money). Owen and his heirs lived there until 1645, when the building suffered extensive damage in the Civil War. Abandoned, it soon began to crumble, and its stones were cannibalised by local builders. The roofless, melancholy ruins are still there today.

Thame Abbey was gobbled up by the town's most powerful occupant, John

Williams, 1st Baron Williams of Thame, Treasurer of the King's Jewels, Lord Chamberlain of England, Lord President of the Council of the Welsh Marches, and one-time High Sheriff of Berkshire and Oxfordshire. He was also reputedly a third cousin to Edward VI, Mary I and Elizabeth I. Williams' job as Treasurer of the King's Jewels meant he was partly in charge of the dissolution, and he scooped up Thame Abbey and its lands. The abbot's house was converted by Williams into a country house.

Other victims of the dissolution included the religious houses at Bicester, Burford, Clattercote, Eynsham, Goring, Studley and Wroxton. Many churches were plundered too, a prime example being the shrine of Our Lady at Caversham, which had been a popular place of pilgrimage. Henry VIII's first wife Katherine of Aragon had visited in July 1532 to pray to the Virgin while Henry was causing chaos in his pursuit of a divorce.

The shrine included a silver-plated statue of the miracle-working virgin. The Mary-onette was dressed in clothes, cap, wig, and a crown made from 20lbs of gold left in the 1439 will of Isabella Beauchamp, Countess of Warwick. This was just the sort of thing that stood no chance of surviving the anti-idolatry Reformation.

Henry's icon-busting henchman Dr John London descended on Caversham in 1538, destroying 'many pretty relics', and sending the Virgin's statue to London to be burnt. It was not until 1958 that the shrine, refitted and re-consecrated, reopened to pilgrims, complete with a new statue of the Virgin. Well, it wasn't *that* new – it was a 500-year-old relic from Northern Europe, supposedly discovered in a London antique shop. The statue was completed in 1996, when a specially made gold and silver crown was placed on its head.

Because of its roots in the Catholic Church and its long history of teachers associated with the friaries and abbeys, Oxford University was worried, initially, that the dissolution would mean its own downfall. Henry ordered the university to debate the issue of the legality of his divorce and remarriage in 1530, and the canny academics returned a suitably philosophical and evasive reply. In the end, the seismic shifts of the dissolution brought great bounty to Oxford, with many colleges buying land formerly held by religious institutions, and new colleges being founded with the dubious profits.

Anthony Wood records tantalisingly that in 1543, 'The King's coming to Oxon was much expected this year, but he came not.' When he did bother turning up, it was Woodstock rather than Oxford that he favoured, on account of the royal hunting park there. Wood also notes that on one occasion Henry installed himself at Woodstock, 'and there an attempt was made on his life by William Morisco'. (Morisco is said to have turned to piracy after this, basing himself in Ireland, before being captured and executed. However, some sources say this happened in the reign of Henry III, and it is possible that Anthony Wood muddled his sources.)

Wood also wrote of a gentler, post-Henry royal visit:

On the 15th of July 1548 ... Queen Catherine (Widow of Henry the VIII) [Catherine Parr] was, with great solemnity, received into Magdalen College, by the Vice Chancellor and Scholars of the University, especially by the Venerable Dr. Owen Oglethorpe, President, with the Scholars of that College, and there entertained with a most sumptuous Banquet, to the great honour of that Society.

OXFORD UNIVERSITY
UNDER THE EARLY TUDORS

In the 1530s the king's commissioners reported gleefully that the library at New College had been trashed. The books, of Catholic origin, were deemed 'superstitious' and therefore evil or, at best, worthless. Many were associated with one of the thirteenth century's leading academics, John Duns Scotus, referred to by Thomas Cromwell's right-hand man Richard Layton as 'Dunce'. The books were ripped apart and thrown into the college quad. Commissioner Layton was able to report:

> We have set Dunce in Bocardo, and utterly banished him from Oxford forever, with all his blind glosses ... The second time we came to New College we found all the great quadrant full of leaves of Dunce, the wind blowing them into every corner. And there we found a certain Mr Greenfield, a gentleman of Buckinghamshire, gathering up part of the said book leaves, as he said, therewith to make him sewells or blanchers, to keep the deer within the wood, thereby to have the better cry with his hounds.

('Sewells' and 'blanchers' are old words for scarecrow-like items placed in a wood to prevent deer from accessing certain areas. Greenfield's ill-gotten harvest of 'leaves' would have been parchment.)

The vandalism continued across the university. Many manuscripts were piled onto bonfires. Anything depicting angels was torched, as these were now viewed as diabolical, Catholic, or both. From Merton College alone a full cartload of manuscripts was removed. A Dutch man called Herks rescued some, and these were later parked in the Bodleian Library.

The librarian at Balliol, a man called Persons, sold most of the college's old books in order to purchase new Protestant ones. Some collections were sold for wastepaper at the price of 40s per library (about £850 in today's money).

By the time Edward VI (1537–1553) was on the throne, most librarians were out of work. Books were associated with worldliness and idolatry, and this served to undermine the whole principle of libraries in Oxford. As Andrew Lang put it, writing in the nineteenth century:

> Oxford was almost empty. The schools were used by laundresses as a place wherein clothes might conveniently be dried. The citizens encroached on academic property. Some schools were quite destroyed, and the sites converted into gardens. The college plate and jewels left by pious benefactors were stolen, and went to the melting pot. Thus flourished Oxford under Edward VI.

BANBURY: THE 'OTHER PLACE'?

In Oxfordshire, higher education meant Oxford. The academic institution there cast a long shadow across the whole island, and combined with the 'Other Place' at Cambridge, academia was in the Oxbridge grip – a monopoly that would not be broken until the nineteenth century.

However, Banbury managed to get more than just a footnote in the history of Oxfordshire education, with the arrival of John Stanbridge in 1501. Born in Adderbury and educated at New College, and a former teacher at Magdalen College School in Oxford, he was elected as schoolmaster by Banbury's St John's Hospital (on the road to Adderbury and Oxford, not too far from the modern Horton General Hospital). Stanbridge was a scholar of the highest calibre, and he wrote what was probably the first book of Latin grammar in the English language. He pulled together existing late-medieval grammars and filtered them through the Renaissance humanist approach of the time. The book, *Accidence*, is written in an easy-to-grasp question and answer format.

Not only did he write the book, Stanbridge applied its teaching principles to the school, single-handedly changing the way Latin and other subjects were taught. His methods became the template in other English schools, and then the norm. His methods spread quickly – in 1515 the statutes of Manchester Free Grammar School stated that schoolmasters were to 'teach children grammar after the school use, manner and form of the school of Banbury ... called Stanbridge grammar'. His texts were used in many other schools too, including Eton, Winchester and St Paul's in London.

According to seventeenth-century historian Anthony Wood, John Stanbridge 'lived poor and bare to his last, yet with a juvenile and cheerful spirit'. This suggests an early manifestation of the puritanical spirit for which Banbury later became synonymous. It was one of the keenest champions of Protestantism in the latter part of the sixteenth century, and the tag 'a Banbury man' came to mean a Puritan.

Banbury's Hospital and School of St John were dissolved in 1549, under the Chantries Act, which sought to close these Catholic-derived institutions. The county's other schools were closed down too, the chief of these being at Burford, Chipping Norton, Deddington, Ewelme, Henley and Witney. Banbury was removed from the portfolio of the Bishops of Lincoln shortly afterwards and taken over by the Crown, becoming a self-governing borough in 1554. The old school was re-founded around this time (and the ones at Ewelme and Chipping Norton, along with Magdalen College School in Oxford, somehow managed to slip through the loophole too).

In 1556 a former pupil of Banbury's St John's School, Sir Thomas Pope of Deddington, nominated the institution as a feeder school for Trinity College. Pope had founded this college in the previous year as 'The College of the Holy and Undivided Trinity in the University of Oxford, of the foundation of Sir Thomas Pope (Knight)'. The source of his wealth was the dissolution of the monasteries. He had been responsible for sorting out the confiscated lands of smaller religious establishments, and much of that sorting out involved assuming the manors and lands for himself. According to eighteenth-century historian John Aubrey, 'He could have rode in his owne lands from Cogges (by Witney) to Banbury, about 18 miles.'

The need for good schools did not disappear, of course, even though most of the schools themselves did. By the 1570s the new grammar school wave was washing over the country, and in Oxfordshire new institutions sprang up in many places, the earliest batch including Adderbury, Thame, Williamscott and Woodstock.

In 1580 the county's first charity school was opened at Somerton. This was a free school set up for the basic education of families with low incomes. It was unique for many decades, going about its business in the shadow of the grammar schools, very much like the early mammals putting down their genetic roots in the long age of the dinosaurs. By the early eighteenth century, the grammars were crumbling, physically and academically, and the age of the elementary, free and charity school was upon us. Somerton went about its business with a well-deserved air of 'I told you so'.

One of the earliest and best of the new crop of charity schools was in Banbury – the Blue Coat School, founded in 1705. Fifty pupils attended at any given time, in schoolrooms enjoying an unprepossessing location above the town gaol.

EDWARD VI
AND THE OXFORDSHIRE UPRISING

Just when things seemed to be calming down, in 1549 the Anglican Church under boy king Edward VI kicked up a storm by imposing the first Act of Uniformity, which imposed the English prayer book on every church in the land. Latin had always been the language of English Christianity, and for many clergymen it was a reform too far. The book was prepared primarily by Thomas Cranmer, who had been ordained Archbishop of Canterbury in 1533.

On Whit Sunday 1549 the people of Bicester rose up in mass protest. The town had felt slighted by Henry VIII's dissolution of the monasteries and the Reformation, losing its priory in the process. But the English language prayer book, cooked up by Edward VI's team, led by Cranmer, was the last straw. The unrest escalated into what is now known as the Oxfordshire and Buckinghamshire Uprising.

Tradition places the decisive confrontation at Enslow Hill on the Cherwell, where the rebels were persuaded to depart in peace with hollow assurances that they would not be harmed. A surviving letter from Lord Grey states that the perpetrators of the unrest are to be executed 'immediately, or else on the next market day ... and after execution done, the heads of every one of them ... to be set up in the highest place for the more terror of the said evil people'.

Bicester's chief miscreant, hanged in public, was Richard Whyttington, a weaver. Three were hanged in Oxford, three in Banbury, and two at Thame, along with single ringleaders at Watlington, Islip and Deddington. The vicars of Chipping Norton and Bloxham were hanged upon their own church steeples. James Webbe, vicar of Barford St Michael, was tried in London, and then hanged, drawn and quartered in Aylesbury.

A letter written in Oxford on 7 August by one John Ab Ulmis confirms the status quo: 'The Oxfordshire papists are at last reduced to order, many of them having been apprehended, and some gibbeted and their heads fastened to the walls.'

THE WYATT REBELLION

In 1554 Sir Thomas Wyatt and four other noblemen led an abortive rebellion to oust Queen Mary and install her sister Elizabeth. The chief problem wasn't Mary's Catholicism per se, but the fact that she was going to consolidate it by marrying the Spanish king, Philip II. They had an alternative royal wedding planned, intending to marry Elizabeth to Edward Courtenay, the 1st Earl of Devon (Elizabeth and Mary's second cousin, through Edward IV).

The plan ground to a halt when the citizens of London routed the rebels, and Wyatt and several others were executed. Elizabeth was promptly arrested and taken to Woodstock under house arrest. Embarrassingly, Woodstock Manor was found to be too dilapidated to accommodate her, and she had to be locked in the gatehouse instead.

A MARTYR OF LIFE OR DEATH

The religious merry-go-round of the sixteenth century produced many martyrs, with Henry VIII, Edward VI, Mary and Elizabeth all sending their unfair share of unrepentant zealots to the noose and flames. Some of the most celebrated of these martyrs were executed in Oxford.

Thomas Cranmer, Archbishop of Canterbury, had been at the controversial edge of Church politics for many years. He was chief architect of Henry VIII's divorce from his first wife Katherine of Aragon and his subsequent marriage to Anne Boleyn. He found himself masterminding the biggest divorce of them all – the English Reformation, in which the country cast itself adrift after 900 years sailing on the See of Rome, launching a homemade version, the Church of England.

When Catholic 'Bloody' Mary I ascended in 1555, Cranmer was doomed. In October 1555 he was condemned to death, along with bishops Hugh Latimer and Nicholas Ridley. They were imprisoned in Oxford's Bocardo Prison, but still refused to recant. Latimer and Ridley went to the flames first, Ridley reassuring his friend that God would either lessen the agony of the flames, or bolster their spirits to withstand the pain. Latimer, reassured, told his companion at the bonfire:

'Be of good cheer, Ridley, and play the man. We shall this day, by God's grace, light up such a candle in England, as I trust, will never be put out.' They were burned in the town ditch at Oxford, at a spot which is now in the middle of Broad Street.

But it was Cranmer's death in March 1556, at the age of 67, that produced the most striking image for local legend. The deposed archbishop had eventually recanted during his two-year imprisonment, in a moment of weakness; but facing the flames he now renounced the signature he had given in an attempt to save his life, declaring: 'This is the hand that wrote it, and therefore shall it suffer first punishment.' As the fire mounted, Cranmer allowed his right hand to burn, shouting, 'This hand hath offended!' throughout the ordeal.

The execution of Latimer and Ridley, from Foxe's *Book of Martyrs*, 1563.

Mary died in 1558, and Protestant Elizabeth I came to the throne. Not much had changed, though, in terms of religious intolerance. In 1581 Edmund Campion, a leading recusant (a term for those who had refused to abandon Catholicism), was unearthed in hidden chambers at Lyford Grange Manor in Oxfordshire along with fellow priests. He had fled here from another recusant stronghold at Stonor Park in the same county, where he printed and distributed Catholic tracts, 400 copies of his 'Ten Reasons' (arguments against Anglicanism) turning up on the pews of St Mary's in Oxford one Sunday morning in 1581.

The captured Campion was driven through Oxford, where he was greeted by many as a hero. He was a fellow of St John's College, and had led a debate there in front of Elizabeth in happier times. She had voiced her high regard for the man; but the former affections of Elizabeth and the university were not enough to save him. He was tried, tortured, hanged, drawn and quartered at Tyburn in London.

In 1589 four more priests, George Nichols, Richard Yaxley, Thomas Belson and Humphrey Pritchard, were executed in Oxford. The site on Holywell Street is marked today with a plaque, as a kind of Catholic rejoinder to the commemorative plaque to Cranmer et al., at the other end of Broad Street.

There were recusants in many parts of Oxfordshire. The Eyston family were foremost among them. They had lived at Hendred House in East Hendred since the fifteenth century, and survived in spite of being quite openly Catholic. Hendred House's private chapel of St Amand and St John the Baptist has been in continuous use as a Catholic church since it was first built in the thirteenth century – a possibly unique achievement in England.

On the Buckinghamshire border at Godington the Catholics outnumbered the Protestants, even in the mid-eighteenth century. They gathered at the chapel of the local Fermor family in Tusmore Park, and later in a converted loft at the Moat House beside the parish church. Other strongholds of the old religion existed at Somerton near Bicester and Shirburn Castle.

QUEEN ELIZABETH'S SAUCY BOYS

Elizabeth I was the first monarch to receive a monetary gift from the university when she visited in 1566. She was presented with a silver cup worth £10, containing £40 in gold (a combined value of about £6,000 in today's money). Prior to this visit, monarchs had been given traditional gifts such as oxen, sheep, lambs, veal calves and loaves of sugar.

The purpose of Elizabeth's visit was to impress on the town the resolute character of the queen, particularly in matters of religious inclinations. She was here to stamp Anglican Protestantism on the city, and to purge Catholicism and the equally troublesome Puritanism. In her own words: 'I mean to let the scholars see that I am not in the humour to stand any nonsense.'

The university did its best to encourage the right kind of nonsense, pasting odes to her beauty on the gates and walls of the colleges, in Latin and Greek. Elizabeth stopped to read these, and is said to have loved them. Young scholars flocked around the queen, bowing gallantly and making witty remarks. They managed to appeal to Elizabeth's playful side, and, according to John Cordy Jeafferson in *Annals of Oxford*, she 'laughingly told them that they were saucy boys, who needed much more whipping than they got from their tutors'. Some of them received kisses and tips.

In Christ Church Hall things went awry when the performance of a new play – *Palamon and Arcyte* by Richard Edwards – was marred by a collapsing stage, which killed three and injured five. But the corpses were simply removed, and the show went on (amidst much applause, we are told). Part two of the play went ahead the following night without incident. The most memorable scene involved a fox hunt: a large group of people had been placed in the Great Quadrangle to impersonate the sounds of the hunt, and students inside the hall joined in the make-believe by cheering the hounds. Elizabeth found this all highly amusing, declaring: 'Oh excellent! Those boys in very truth are ready to leap out of the windows to follow the hounds!'

Playwright Edwards must have thought his theatrical and financial boat had come in after this royal thumbs-up. Unfortunately, he died a couple of months later.

The queen revisited the city in 1592, and was apparently far less agreeable in her relative old age.

ROAD TO RUIN

The roads in the south of England up until the second half of the Tudor period were notoriously bad. After heavey rain they became impassable trenches of mud, and were often abandoned until the land dried out. Settlements could be completely cut off in these conditions. But by the time Elizabeth came to the throne, many towns and villages in Oxfordshire had been forced to do something about it.

Parliament passed laws in 1555 requiring parishes to take responsibility for the state of their roads, and surveyors were employed to report on each major thoroughfare. Parishioners had a new tithe to pay, in the form of carts, oxen or horses and road materials, along with several hours of their time, to help fix the local quagmire that was supposed to be a road.

It was an unpopular policy, and many simply refused to comply with the demands on their time and resources. They might well be fined, but that was often less of a burden on them than the time lost in carrying out roadworks. As an illustration of this, in 1576 the roads to Oxford, and the relevant bridges, were in such a bad state – in spite of the supposed improvements – that farmers and tradesmen could not get their goods to market there.

The situation remained dire for another 200 years, when the Turnpike Acts gave England its first decent roads since the Roman era.

WILLIAM DAVENANT: SHAKESPEARE JUNIOR

William Davenant of Oxford claimed that he was the illegitimate son of William Shakespeare. The Bard is thought to have regularly lodged in the city en route from Stratford to London, staying with his friend John Davenant, wine merchant, sometime Mayor of Oxford and keeper of The Bull Inn (in the still-standing building at 3 Cornmarket). He is even said to have penned *The Winter's Tale* here in 1610.

William Davenant, who was himself a playwright, was happy to concur with a piece of handy folklore regarding Shakespeare's fondness for his mother, Jane Shepherd

Davenant. For a dramatist it was an association of the very highest calibre.

Shakespeare is said to have been godfather to baby William at St Martin's, Carfax, in 1606. It is possible that Jane was seeking respite from her downbeat husband: according to seventeenth-century historian Anthony Wood, Davenant senior 'was a very grave and discreet citizen (yet an admirer of plays and playmakers, especially Shakespeare, who frequented his house in his journeys between Warwickshire and London), was of a melancholic disposition, and was seldom or never known to laugh'.

PURITANISM COMES EARLY TO BANBURY

Puritanism found its most extreme outlet in Banbury, spurred on by the parliamentary ranting of its MP Sir Anthony Cope of Hanwell. He had pulled down the maypole at Neithrop, after winning a court case following a Puritan-versus-May-Day revellers' riot in 1589. The Puritans believed that all images relating to Christianity were idolatrous vestiges of Catholicism and paganism. With all the town's churches stripped to a pleasing grey, the only villains left were Banbury's crosses.

Chief target was the fifteenth-century High Cross or Market Cross, in Cornhill off the Market Place. Pretty and innocuous to many, it was a symbol of idolatry to others; and a gang of Puritans led by William Knight, Richard Wheatley, Thomas Wheatley and Henry Shewell toppled it in 1600. At the inquest that followed, anti-Puritan observer Matthew Knight said he had seen the men, in a company of more than 150, hack at the cross with axes:

William Knight with a great voice did encourage and animate the said workman saying, 'Come let us down with it and down with it quickly', and presently the spire of the said high cross did fall to the ground to the great discontentment of many that were present. The said Shewell cried out, 'God be thanked, their god Dagon is fallen down to the ground!'

The town's Bread Cross, at the corner of High Street and Butcher's Row, suffered the same fate. It had been a very practical structure, with a slate roof offering shelter for the bread and meat stalls that used to trade there, and with a Good Friday bread dole handed out there annually.

A third structure, the White Cross, a boundary cross situated at what is now the corner of West Bar Street and Beargarden Road, seems to have survived the vandalism.

(The modern cross, dominating the crossroads in the centre of the town, was erected in 1859 to mark the marriage of Queen Victoria's eldest daughter Victoria Adelaide Mary Louisa to Friedrich Wilhelm of Prussia.)

THE OXFORD RISING

In 1592, as part of her itinerary through Oxfordshire, Elizabeth I visited Sir Henry Lee, former Queen's Champion and MC at her accession festivities, at his house in Ditchley. Lee staged an old-fashioned two-day spectacle of tilting, chivalric pursuits and other fripperies.

Fast forward to 1596 … Ditchley is now a deserted village, enclosures having robbed the villagers of their resources, compounded by 1596's poor harvests and corresponding high prices. Bartholomew Steer, a carpenter from Hampton Poyle, leads the anti-enclosure Oxfordshire

Rising, planning a visit to the former Queen's Champion Henry Lee, along with other rich property owners of the region, with the intention of beheading them and then marching to London as part of a larger rebellion.

The rising was soon crushed. John Barry, lord of the manor of Hampton Gay, was tipped off by a local carpenter, possibly wishing to see the competition axed, literally. The Oxfordshire Rising's ringleaders were arrested, and Steer was sentenced to be hanged, drawn and quartered.

The rising wasn't without positive repercussions, however: it led directly to the Tillage Act of 1597 which restored much arable land lost to pasture. Parliament stated that 'order should be taken about inclosures … that the poor may be able to live'.

Fine words, but with little impact on the juggernaut of the enclosure movement in the long run. The enclosures continued through the next three centuries, inexorably barring the commoners from the commons.

7

THE STUARTS
1603–1714

The seventeenth century was Britain's age of revolution, and many of the key events took place in Oxfordshire.

The accession of King James I was marked by plague. It started in London in 1603 and soon spread to Oxford. Most students fled, and the Michaelmas term had to be cancelled. All college gates were locked, shops were closed, even cats and dogs vanished from the streets, and grass is said to have grown in the thoroughfares.

JAMES I, THE WHITEWASHED SUN KING

When King James I visited the Bodleian Library Schools Quad on his first Oxford visit in 1603, the sun was blazing, which seemed an auspicious sign. But James was nothing if not contrary, and, complaining that the gold gilt on the figures in the quad dazzled him, he ordered them to be 'whitened over'. Ironically, the creators of the King James Bible (written at his command) compared James to the rising sun in all its glory. Detractors muttered that he was more like a bucket of whitewash.

James' effigy still sits above the gateway, holding the famous Bible that became the voice and poetry of the Anglican Church for the next 350 years. Folklore maintains that this Bible fell from James' stony hand in 1865 when William Gladstone, prime minister and Christ Church alumnus, lost his University of Oxford parliamentary seat.

In 1604 James I came back to Oxford to personally investigate the strange case of a preacher called Richard Haydock, a fellow of New College. James' mission was to sniff out witchcraft, a subject in which he had a great interest, and on which he had written a treatise, *Daemonologie*, in 1597.

Haydock had acquired national fame as a preacher; but he claimed that his sermons only came to him in his sleep. By day he could barely string two sentences together, due to a bad stammer, but he become a celebrity due to his divinely inspired sleep-sermons.

It turned out to be a scam, not surprisingly – a simple means of getting money from the crowds who came to witness his sleep-sermons. But the fame that the hoax brought him caught the ears of the new king. A conviction of witchcraft carried the sentence of death. So, sensing doom, Haydock confessed. He wasn't really asleep, he admitted, but had carefully planned the sermons and learnt them by heart. It wasn't an easy ruse – his listeners would often pinch and slap him, to check if he was really asleep; but Haydock always made it to the end of his speeches, in spite of the audience intervention.

It was when summoned before James for a private sleep-preaching session at New College that Haydock caved in and confessed. He had wanted the attention, he said, because he felt himself 'a buried man at the University'. Speaking in bed with his eyes closed enabled him to escape his stammer, and he had started out innocently enough by writing sermons and then trying to recall them in his dreams.

James was unusually lenient, ordering Haydock to make his confession public, but leaving it at that. In gratitude, Haydock composed a treatise on dreams and dedicated it to the demon-hunting king.

John Clavell also had cause to breathe a sigh of relief. He wrote the poem *A Recantation of an Ill Led Life* in prison while under sentence of death for highway robbery, and sent it to King James, in hope of a royal pardon. Clavell had studied at Brasenose between 1619 and 1621, but never took his degree. In April 1621 he narrowly avoided imprisonment after stealing some of the college's silver; but mounting debts persuaded him that being a highwayman was the best option, until he was captured in 1626.

Surprisingly, Clavell's poem caught James in a mood of clemency once again, and the death penalty was lifted. By the 1630s he was working as a lawyer and physician in Ireland.

Another man who did well after a poor start was Timothy Tyrell, Master of the Buckhounds to King James I's eldest son, Prince Henry. After a hunt in Shotover Forest, Timothy held the head of a deer so that the prince could kill it; but in cutting its throat Henry's blade slipped. Tyrell's hand was wounded so badly that he was permanently maimed. In compensation he received a grant, in 1613, of lands at Shotover; and he was knighted there in 1624. Henry did less well, dying in 1612, aged 18.

EARLY CASUALTIES OF WAR

One of the first Oxfordshire men to plough a furrow that led directly to the English Civil War was William Fiennes. As Viscount Saye and Sele of Broughton, he was one of Oxfordshire's foremost aristocrats. He also had a huge house – Broughton Castle, home of Lord and Lady Saye and Sele and the Fiennes family from the early fourteenth century to the present day – to entertain like-minded Parliamentarian guests.

William Fiennes had been imprisoned by James I in 1622 for speaking out against the king's inept policies and high taxes. Among Fiennes' friends gathering at Broughton Castle to plan a challenge to the royal whims of James' successor Charles I were John Hampden, John Pym, Sir Henry Vane and Robert Devereux, the Earl of Essex. These men were central figures in the Civil Wars to come. They nicknamed William Fiennes 'Old Subtlety', as he always managed to keep his political arguments within the law, rather than calling for sedition. Broughton was later captured by the Royalists, but Fiennes kept his head, both literally and metaphorically.

It is said that Oliver Cromwell planned Edgehill, the first major battle of the Civil War, from his Banbury rooms in The Rein Deer (now Ye Olde Rein Deer Inn). The battle, fought in October 1642, was won convincingly by the Royalists in spite of all Cromwell's long nights in the pub.

In 1643 Oxfordshire was initially in the grip of the Royalists. Their bases included Abingdon, Banbury, Boarstall, Burford, Chipping Norton, Faringdon, Shirburn, Wallingford and Woodstock. They also commanded some key river crossings, including Islip Bridge, Radcot Bridge and Wheatley Bridge. The Parliamentarians made many inroads over the next two years, but initially their main strongholds in the county were Chinnor, Henley, Tetsworth, Thame and Watlington, with a larger host not too far away at Reading.

In many places it was tit-for-tat. The Parliamentarians took Mapledurham House by force, as a gesture against its Royalist owner Sir Charles Blount; while at Shirburn, landowner Sir John Chamberlain made it a condition of tenants' leases that they should support the Royalist army if called to do so.

As with any polarising debate, the Civil War left communities, and even families, divided. Henry Danvers of Cornbury Park, for example, was a pro-Royalist who had gifted King Charles £3,400 (worth around £400,000 in today's money), and tied up loopholes in his will so that his pro-Parliamentarian brother would not inherit any of the estate.

The church at Radley near Abingdon was battered during a skirmish when Parliamentarians were trying to winkle out the Royalists in and around Abingdon, and dents in the door, made by irate locked-out soldiers, can still be seen.

One of Radley church's benefactors, William Lenthall, blew with the winds of the time: he took up the Parliamentarian cause in the wars, and was Speaker on several occasions before, during and after the conflict. He was banned from holding further public office after the Restoration, retiring to his grand piles at Burford Priory and Besselsleigh Manor, dying at the latter on 9 November 1662. His on-the-fence role in history seems to have preyed on his conscience. In his will he requested that he be buried with neither pomp nor monument, 'acknowledging myself to be unworthy of the least outward regard in this world and unworthy of any remembrance that hath been so great a sinner'. Instead he asked for a plain stone carved with the Latin inscription *Vermis sum*, meaning 'I am a worm'.

Another victim of the war was the bell tower of All Saints in Faringdon, damaged by a Parliamentarian cannonball. Faringdon was a key strategic spot on the road to the Radcot Bridge over the Thames, and worth fighting for. The Royalists, holed up at Faringdon House, managed to retain control. The house was damaged too, with its owner at the time, Sir Robert Pye, under siege from his own son Robert, a Parliamentarian colonel. The church tower was partially demolished in 1645, and Faringdon House was rebuilt in the eighteenth century.

WAR HQ OXFORD

In 1643 Oxford swapped its academic robes for the trappings of war, with schools turned overnight into army barracks, students ousted by soldiers, and flocks in the surrounding fields displaced by cannons.

Royalist the city may have been, but not everyone was overjoyed at Charles I's decision to base himself in Oxford. New College was transformed into an army warehouse of munitions and hardware, while Oriel became a foundry producing cannons, and housing the king's Privy Council. The mill at Osney ground gunpowder instead of flour. New Inn Hall became the Oxford Mint, producing coinage to pay the army, using melted-down college plate and other metal ware purloined from university and household alike. The new University Schools became stores for foodstuffs and workshops for clothing and other necessities.

To make things even more tense, the inhabitants of Oxford were heavily taxed to finance the king's military takeover, and all men aged between 16 and 45 were forced to enlist in the Royalist army. A darkly symbolic gibbet was erected at Carfax, while the plague that proceeded to rage through the populace simply added insult to injury.

The Royalists had a garrison at Culham Bridge as part of their Abingdon encampment. But in 1644 the Parliamentarians gained control of Abingdon, a strategically crucial base from which they could attack Royalist supply lines into Oxford. At the Battle of Culham Bridge on 11 January 1645 the Royalists tried and failed to blow up the bridge, and their commander Sir Henry Gage died of injuries inflicted during the attempt.

Oxfordshire was now the eye of the Civil War storm, the king's base at Oxford lying just 8 miles from Abingdon.

THE BATTLE OF CHALGROVE

In 1643 Royalist Prince Rupert harried Roundhead garrisons at Chinnor and Postcombe, razing the villages and taking prisoners and booty. In response the Parliamentarians sent an army from their base in Thame to confront Rupert.

On 18 June the Royalists rode to Chalgrove, and Rupert guaranteed his place in the history books by leading his cavalry, and his pet dog Boy, in an ambush over a high hedge and on to victory at the Battle of Chalgrove Field. He captured eighty officers and paraded them through Oxford. Many other Roundhead generals had been killed in the battle. One of them was John Hampden – levelling his pistol at the enemy, the weapon had exploded in his hand, mortally wounding him.

There were several other Oxfordshire confrontations. A plaque on the bridge in Cropredy reads: 'Site of the Battle of Cropredy Bridge. From Civil War deliver us'. The battle took place on 29 June 1644, and William Waller's Parliamentarians suffered heavy losses; but like many skirmishes the conflict ended with no clear winner.

At Cuddesdon the Bishop of Oxford's palace was burnt down by retreating Royalists in 1645 to prevent it being occupied by the enemy. It had only been completed ten years earlier. The main building at Godstow nunnery, which had been converted to a private house, was pulled down too, for similar reasons.

ANTHONY WOOD'S CIVIL WAR

Historian and war witness Anthony Wood notes how in 1643 Robert Devereux, Earl of Essex and 'Generalissimo of the Parliament Forces', came from Abingdon, over Sandford Ferry, on his way to nearby Islip. As his host came close to the city walls, Wood says Essex and his men stopped and conferred.

Wood's mother was pretty certain this meant imminent war, and because of the added hazards of the plague outbreak, she sent Anthony and his brother to the relative safety of Thame. It was certainly not immune to the effects of the war, though, with its grammar school temporarily functioning as a garrison and hospital. Anthony Wood wrote:

> While A. Wood and his brother Christopher continued at Thame, you cannot imagine what great disturbances they suffered by the Soldiers of both parties, sometimes by the Parliament soldiers

of Aylesbury, sometimes by the King's from Borstall house, and sometimes from the King's at Oxon. and at Wallingford.

The diarist tells of Royalist colonel Thomas Blagge, governor of Wallingford, retreating on horseback from a skirmish at Long Crendon via Thame, passing by the house where the young man was staying. Fifty Parliamentarians were in hot pursuit: Blagge raced by, his face all cut and bloodied; and one of his men, heading up the sloping bank opposite Wood's door, was thrown by his panicking horse. One of the enemy aimed a pistol at him, 'but the trooper crying Quarter, the Rebels came up, rifled him, and took him and his horse away with them. Crawford [Lawrence Crawford, colonel, and governor of the Aylesbury garrison] rode on without touching him, and ever or anon he would be discharging his pistol at some of the fag-end of Blagge's horse, who rode thro the West end of Thame ... towards Ricot.' Crafford ended the pursuit here, retiring to a local inn instead.

On 7 September 1645 William Legge, Royalist governor of Oxford, led 400 horsemen and sixty musketeers from the city with his brother, High Sheriff of Oxfordshire, David Walter. Their aim was to arrest Parliamentarians in Thame. Wood says the mustering was so sudden and so early that some Oxford men rode forth in their nightshirts. Wood wrote: 'the two gallant majors charged the Rebels up thro the Street, doing execution all the way to the Market-place, where ... [they] gave the Rebels such a charge as made them fly out of the Town'. The regrouped rebels attacked the Royalists as they made their way back to Oxford, killing a few in the process.

THE SIEGE OF OXFORD

In May 1644 there were some minor skirmishes at Headington Hill and St Clements, where cannon were fired while King Charles watched from Magdalen bell tower. The Parliamentarians under the command of the Earl of Essex made camp at Islip. By June they were ready to attack Oxford.

The Royalists had abandoned their bases at Woodstock and elsewhere in the vicinity and gathered their full force in Oxford. The provisions they had gathered would only last them fourteen days. With Charles I's safety their first priority, they sent troops to Abingdon as a diversion, while Charles fled from Oxford disguised as his sons' tutor's servant at 9 p.m. on 3 June 1644. The exodus included Prince Charles, a gaggle of courtiers, 2,500 musketeers and all the Royalist cavalry. They passed through Wolvercote, making it to Burford and relative safety seventeen hours later.

The king's absence was not immediately obvious to his enemies. In addition to his Abingdon decoy, Charles had left 3,500 infantry in north Oxford, their cannon trained on the besiegers. William Waller, late in the day, eventually saw through the ruse and hurtled after the king's train, managing to cut down a few Royalist tail-enders at Burford. But Charles hadn't paused, and was soon safe in Royalist Worcester.

Essex and Waller were taken off duty, and General Sir Richard Browne was put in charge of the Oxford campaign. His mission was to take not just Oxford, but Banbury and Wallingford too, and Oliver Cromwell's New Model Army declared the seizure of Oxford its number one priority. Cromwell and General Browne were stationed just beyond the city walls, and on 23 May 1645 the committee of the army was given the go-ahead by the House of Commons to raise 'such money and necessaries for the Siege of Oxford'.

General Thomas Fairfax blocked up all routes of escape, with the opposing forces occupying different Oxford suburbs. River crossings were guarded, all outlying houses were commandeered, and the Royalists torched a few houses in their retreat to Wolvercote in the north. Fairfax watched from the frontline, literally dodging bullets on one occasion, while in a show of strength his cannon proved how far it could penetrate the enemy ranks when a ball was fired from Marston to the walls of Christ Church a mile away.

Just before sunrise on 2 June, the Royalists made a surprise attack on Headington Hill, killing fifty of Fairfax's besiegers, wounding many more and taking ninety-six prisoners. Fairfax arranged an exchange of prisoners and called a temporary halt to the siege.

THE SURRENDER OF OXFORD

In November 1645, in the absence of a decisive blow from either side, King Charles decided to spend another winter in Oxford. The siege was still in recess, but the Parliamentarians were firmly entrenched in the vicinity, their military mastermind Thomas Fairfax installed at 17 Mill Lane in Marston. Now known as Cromwell House, this building was to be the scene of negotiations over the long-drawn-out Treaty of Oxford.

When Charles arrived on 5 November, his cause was very much on the wane. Former wonder kid

Prince Rupert was now just another besieged soldier in Oxford, his star having faded after he was routed at the Battle of Marston Moor near York on 2 July 1644. Charles' only hopes now lay with reinforcements. Troops had been promised from Scotland, but they would take several days to arrive. Disastrously, his Welsh and Worcester reinforcements were defeated at Stow-on-the-Wold.

Meanwhile, the New Model Army was ordered to 'straiten' Oxford; but the Royalists refused to lie down. Troops clashed in Woodstock, and the noise of their cannon fire on 15 April 1646 could be heard in Oxford. When Parliamentarians under Thomas Rainsborough attacked Woodstock Manor House, they were beaten back with surprising ease. More than 100 of Rainsborough's men were killed in the battle, with many more wounded. But the Woodstock siege continued, and on 26 April the manor house fell to the Parliamentarians, its governor and his army fleeing to Oxford, weaponless.

Charles, meanwhile, was preparing to escape from Oxford in disguise once again. The Oxford Mint managed to forge Thomas Fairfax's official seal, and using this token Charles made it as far as London, adopting the on-the-road name Harry.

On 1 May 1646 Fairfax sent in the army. He had spied on the Royalist defences and artillery in the University Parks from a vantage point on the top of St Nicholas' church in Marston, so he knew exactly what to expect. His army occupied all key villages around the city, establishing HQ at Headington. Three thousand men were stationed at Headington Hill, with further contingents at Cowley, Elsfield, north Oxford and Marston (where a new bridge was built over the Cherwell). Faringdon, Radcot, Wallingford and Boarstall House were blockaded to prevent them drip-feeding reinforcements to the Oxford Royalists.

Fairfax, after planning tactics with Oliver Cromwell in Marston, arranged his army in a line from the Headington HQ, through St Clements and as far as Magdalen Bridge, just outside the city walls. But Oxford refused to surrender, and on 13 May Fairfax ordered his artillery to fire from Headington Hill, the first shots landing in Christ Church Meadow.

The Royalists were defiant, but on 15 May King Charles' Privy Council in Oxford negotiated a ceasefire, and the house at Mill Lane was nominated as a meeting place for opposing generals to hammer out a treaty of surrender. The officers of the garrison of Oxford were outraged, still convinced they could win the war. They declared that they had not been defeated by Fairfax and Cromwell, but by betrayal from their own commanders. The surrender of Wallingford Castle soon afterwards saw the last Royalist stronghold fall to the now all-conquering Fairfax. The castle was partly demolished, just in case things ever flared up again.

There were a few more skirmishes, but by 10 June Fairfax was sufficiently confident to send a fraternal gift to his enemy the Duke of York (the future James II), who was still holed up in the city. This consisted of 'a Brace of Bucks, two muttons, two veals, two lambs, and six capons'. On 20 June the articles of surrender were finally signed, having been agreed by both sides at Water Eaton. The signing was carried out in the Audit House at Christ Church, the key signatories being the governor of Oxford and triumphant Thomas Fairfax.

THE RETREAT FROM OXFORD

On 22 June 1646 the former hero Prince Rupert, James the Duke of York and 300 high-ranking Royalists were given safe passage from the city, and two days later the treaty came into operation. Fairfax's army patrolled the streets to maintain order, and the Royalist evacuation began, with 3,000 soldiers marching from the city that had not fallen, by military means, in spite of three successive sieges. Anthony Wood writes:

> Wednesday and Midsomer day, the Garrison of Oxon which was the chiefest hold the King had, and wherein he had mostly resided while the Civil War continued, was surrendered for the use of the Parliament, as most of his Garrisons were this year, occasioned by the fatal Battle of Naseby, which happened in the last year, wherein the King and his party were in a woeful manner worsted. In the evening of the said Day, many of the King's Foot-party, that belonged to the Oxon Garrison, came into Thame, and laid down their armes there ... After his return to the house of his Nativity, [Wood] found Oxford empty, as to Scholars, but pretty well replenished with Parliamentarian Soldiers. Many of the Inhabitants had gained great store of wealth from the Court and Royalists, that had for several years continued among them; but as for the young men of the City and University, he found many of them to have been debauched by bearing arms, and doing the duties belonging to soldiers, as watching, warding, and sitting in Tippling-Houses for whole nights together.

The Treaty of Oxford ended the first English Civil War. Round two began in 1648, ending with a final royalist defeat in August 1649. Charles was put on trial for treason. War hero Thomas Fairfax, a constitutional monarchist, took no part in the trial and resigned as head of the army. This enabled Oliver Cromwell to come to the fore.

Charles I was executed on 30 January 1649 at the Palace of Whitehall in London. William Fiennes of Broughton Castle, who had been a thorn in the side of the monarchy since the days of James I, was one of many who did not condone the decision, speaking out strongly against the killing of the king. He retired to his comfy fortress at Broughton, and stayed well out of it until his death in 1662, two months shy of his 80th birthday.

War broke out again that year, when the Scottish Royalists continued the battle against Parliament, with their newly proclaimed King Charles II safely in France. This is sometimes called the third English Civil War, although it is more useful to view it as an Anglo-Scottish war, the first bout in what later became the Jacobite Wars, which reverberated through Oxfordshire – and the rest of the island – two generations later.

The Parliamentarians encountered a lot of opposition from Royalist Oxford University's masters and fellows, and imposed their own men at the institution to quell the ever-simmering rebellion. This was carried out through a process called the Parliamentary Visitation, a political (anti-Royalist) and religious (pro-Presbytarian) purge. The first visitation was in 1647, and they continued for several more years.

Margaret Fell – wife of Royalist Samuel Fell the dean of Christ Church and vice-chancellor of the university – refused to vacate the premises when her husband was ousted, and she was carried bodily into the quadrangle, screaming abuse at the squad of musketeers who man-handled her. Samuel Fell was imprisoned after refusing to appear before the Parliamentary Visitation of April 1648, and was stripped of all his offices. After his release later in the year, he retired to Sunningwell near Abingdon, where he had been rector since 1625.

In that visitation of 1648, only one college head had agreed to appear before the panel – Paul Hood, rector of Lincoln College, who was that very rare university beast, a Puritan sympathiser.

THE LEVELLERS, THE BANBURY MUTINY, AND THE BURFORD MARTYRS

Not all was well in the ranks of Oliver Cromwell's New Model Army, and many disaffected soldiers became involved in the Banbury Mutiny. The initial complaints were against lack of pay, and the men made political demands too, feeling that they deserved a better lot after playing such a vital role in the Parliamentarians' victory in the Civil Wars. This discontent was part of a wider movement centred on the Levellers, who demanded the kind of democracy and representation that eventually came 300 years later.

Four hundred soldiers under the command of Captain William Thompson left their barracks in Banbury to meet with likeminded discontents at Salisbury. Cromwell and Fairfax reassured them that their grievances would be heard, and that their actions so far would not be punished. Cromwell then reneged and attacked the mutineers by night on 13 May 1649. Several were killed, and although William Thompson escaped, he was killed later in a skirmish at Wellingborough.

Quelled, the mutineers, about 340 of them, were briefly imprisoned in Burford church, where traces of their graffiti can still be seen. 'ANTHONY SEDLEY 1649 PRISNER' is one of the most famous pieces of graffiti in the country, inscribed on the lead font. The three perceived leaders of the mutiny, including James Thompson, William Thompson's brother, were executed, and the Leveller movement died with them.

RESTORATION AND DEBAUCHERY

Oxford had remained loyal to the Stuarts, and there were official celebrations to mark the Restoration in 1660 with feasting, fireworks and bell ringing. The Commonwealth college heads were unceremoniously booted out by Charles II. In many cases this was little more than spiteful political gesture, and often bad news for academia. Historian Anthony Wood commented: 'Some Cavaliers that were restored were good scholars, but the majority were dunces.' One of the worst struck was Exeter College, which received Joseph Maynard as its rector. Wood wrote:

> Exeter College is now much debauched by a drunken Governor, whereas, before, in Doctor Conant's time, it was accounted a civil house, it is now rude and uncivil ... The Rector is good-natured, generous and a good scholar, but ... he is much given to bibbing [drinking], and ... he will sit there, smoke, and drink till he is drunk, and has to be led to his lodgings.

Wood was equally scathing when assessing the new breed of Restoration student, complaining: 'Their aim is not to live as students ought to do, but to live like gentry, to keep dogs and horses, to turn their studies into places to keep bottles, to swagger in gay apparel and long periwigs.'

During the Great Plague of London (1665–66), Charles II followed his father's instincts and set up court in Oxford.

During the reign of the supposedly Merry Monarch there was an upwelling of new, bawdy, satirical entertainment taking place, the puritanical cork having well and truly popped. John Wilmot, 2nd Earl of Rochester (1647–1680), was the foremost jester of the times, a writer of scurrilous poetry and drama.

Wilmot was born in Ditchley, educated at Oxford's Wadham College, had a large estate at Adderbury, and later lived at Spelsbury. Precocious, he gained his Master's degree at the age of 14, and was said to have entered into debauchery during those teenage years. This set him up well for a role in Charles II's so-called 'Merry Gang' of court-jesters-cum-hellraisers. He managed to get banished from court a couple of times, once for writing a satire on the king, in which he blamed the monarch's obsession with sex for the sad state of the country.

By 1680 it was all over. A combination of venereal diseases and alcoholism led to Wilmot's death at Woodstock, aged 33. He is buried at Sparsholt, and gained posthumous fame for his supposed deathbed renunciation of atheism and dissoluteness, ordering that his lewd works be gathered up and burnt. None of which prevented his spectacularly obscene play *Sodom, or the Quintessence of Debauchery* from surviving, one rare copy fetching £45,600 at Sotheby's in 2004.

OXFORDSHIRE DISSENT

Charles ousted twenty-six Oxfordshire clergymen as part of his anti-Puritan policy. The chief effect of this purge, however, was to bolster the dissenter movement. Samuel Wells, forced to leave his position at Banbury, became minister at a Presbyterian congregation called the Old Meeting. Congregational churches also opened in Henley, Witney and elsewhere in the early 1660s, and by the close of the century there were several Baptist meeting houses in the county.

Aston Tirrold was one of the county's chief hotbeds of religious dissent and unconformity. Between 1661 and 1665 a series of Acts known as the Clarendon Code (after Charles II's Lord Chancellor Edward Hyde, Earl of Clarendon) had prescribed all the texts and rituals required by practising Anglican clergy. Many ministers refused to fall in line, and at least 2,000 were kicked out of the Church of England, many Oxfordshire men amongst them. They never looked back.

A Presbyterian community was established at Aston Tirrold soon after 1662. The religious freedom this offered was offset by the fact that adherents could not hold any public office or occupy an official religious edifice, or come within 5 miles of their former churches, or of any towns with a corporation, having suffered the Anglican equivalent of an excommunication.

The leading local dissenters were Thomas Cheesman, former vicar of East Garston in Berkshire, and Richard Comyns, erstwhile incumbent of Cholsey. They happily did without churches, preaching to their followers in barns and open spaces, swaying hundreds to their way of thinking via the Society of Dissenters, founded at Aston Tirrold in the late 1660s.

In 1654 the Quakers made their first attempts to convert Oxfordshire, when Elizabeth Heavens and Elizabeth Fletcher preached in Oxford, warning students of their spiritually erring ways. It was hardly something the average student needed reminding of, and the bold Quakers were manhandled to the water pump at St John's College and given a treatment akin to waterboarding. The women almost drowned in the ordeal.

The mayor of Oxford objected to this harsh treatment of the missionaries, but the chancellor of the university was having none of it. He ordered the Elizabeths to be whipped out of the city.

The Quakers soldiered on, though, and often became the local sport of the mob. In Warborough, one church official was said to attend Quaker meetings when drunk, in order to abuse the participants. In Banbury on one occasion the local militia raided a Quaker meeting and beat up those attending. At the more high-brow end of the abuse, William 'Old Subtlety' Fiennes of Broughton Castle wrote abusive pamphlets about the dissenters.

But in spite of all this, they were here to stay, and the Quakers' regular Banbury meeting became a permanent fixture.

JOHN MILTON: NO PARADISE

The poet and Parliamentarian John Milton (1608–74), of *Paradise Lost* fame, got married in 1640 – at Forest Hill, according to local legend. His 16-year-old bride was Mary Powell, daughter of rich Royalist Richard Powell of Forest Hill. But it was not a marriage made in Paradise, and after a few days Mary moved back in with her parents. Four years later she repented and went back to Milton, blaming her mother's snobbery and her father's anti-Parliamentarian views for the cold feet. But it was too late: the flames of love had died, and Milton filed for divorce. This was a fundamental turning point for him, a softening of his previously evangelical Puritanism.

Milton had been a leading intellectual light during the Commonwealth. When Charles II took the throne in 1660, the now-blind poet had every reason to think he might be arrested, along with other high-profile Cromwell supporters. He was, however, saved by William Davenant, godson of William Shakespeare. Davenant had done well from his links to the Bard, becoming Poet Laureate in 1638 and earning the semi-ironic nickname Sweet Swan of Isis (Isis being the name for the Oxford stretch of the River Thames).

Davenant had been a Royalist during the Civil War, in contrast to the Parliamentarian Milton, but they are said to have had a mutual respect based on writing. In 1650 Milton became Secretary of Foreign Tongues, an official mouthpiece, pamphleteer and press censor for the Commonwealth, just as Davenant was heading to prison for high treason. Milton used his influence to get him released.

Forest Hill Church of St Nicholas. (Photo by Magdalena Sullivan)

With Charles II in power, it was now Davenant's turn to play the role of rescuer. He made sure Milton was included on the king's Act of Indemnity and Oblivion, which offered a pardon and blank slate for Cromwell supporters who were not immediately involved with the execution of Charles I.

This return of favour both saved Milton's life and propelled him into the period of poetry writing for which he is now justly famous. At the time of the Restoration he was known solely for his outspoken Puritan pamphlets. He had also supported the execution of Charles I.

Milton had never acted for personal gain. He was a highly moral individual, and hugely intelligent too. Like all intelligent moral people, he changed his views and ideas as the years passed and his wisdom and experience increased. He had, for example, been anti-divorce, until that bitter experience with Mary Powell of Forest Hill.

CHRISTOPHER WREN: BUILDING A REPUTATION

Under the guiding hand of Christopher Wren, this was an era of revolution in architecture. Wren had been educated at Wadham College in Oxford, and later became a fellow of All Souls – one of the greatest distinctions of the university to this day.

While studying at Wadham in the early 1650s, Wren became one of a group of mathematical and philosophical geniuses associated with the Oxford Philosophical Club, run by Wadham's warden John Wilkins. This group was one of the roots of the Royal Society, founded in 1660.

Tom Tower, Christ Church College.

Wren left his mark on Oxford by designing the elaborate sundial at All Souls, whose iconic twin tower frontage was the work of Wren's contemporary Nicholas Hawksmoor (whose work is often wrongly attributed to Wren). The Sheldonian Theatre in Oxford was also Wren's work, as was the design for Tom Tower at Christ Church. Wren did not supervise the erection of the latter, but left it to an architect and stonemason called Christopher Kempster of Burford.

The County Hall building in Abingdon (currently a museum), perched on pillars and arches, was also Kempster's work. He had chiselled his way to expertise under the guidance of Christopher Wren during the building of St Paul's Cathedral in London.

THE GREAT FIRE OF EAST HAGBOURNE

East Hagbourne suffered catastrophe in 1659 when most of its houses were lost in a fire, their thatched roofs the perfect fuel. Charles II was petitioned for aid, and in 1661 money was raised from Londoners and sent to the village to assist the rebuilding. The surviving sturdy, timber-framed buildings from this era are testimony to money well spent.

The recipients were thankful that Charles did not hold a grudge – during the Civil War in 1644 the Parliamentarians had transformed the village into a barracks for 6,000 of its horsemen.

But the story did not end there. In 1666 when London suffered a conflagration of its own, the villagers reciprocated by clubbing together and sending money to help the city rebuild itself.

Fire destroyed the village of Churchill too, which used to lie at the foot of Hastings Hill. Like all other settlements in late seventeenth-century England it was assessed for hearth tax, a levy raised on chimneys. One baker decided to avoid paying by removing his own chimney and linking his hearth to his neighbour's chimney via a crafty connecting hole.

Unfortunately, the single chimney could not take the heat, and on 31 July 1684 it caught fire. Twenty houses were destroyed in the conflagration, and four people roasted. In a drastic rebuilding programme, the village was relocated higher up the hill, with stone used instead of the timber and thatch of the earlier buildings. Lumps in the field around the Heritage Centre indicate where the old village used to be.

300 YEARS OF JETHRO TULL

Agricultural pioneer Jethro Tull of Crowmarsh Gifford invented the horse-drawn seed drill in 1701. His achievement is commemorated on a blue plaque at his cottage on the village's main road. The seed drill was one of the labour- and time-saving innovations at the heart of the Agricultural Revolution, and Tull followed the invention with a horse-drawn hoe, which would enable farmers to phase out the use of oxen.

Tull's interest in a more intensive, scientific approach to farming came after a heart condition had led him to visit Europe in search of a decent doctor. He studied agricultural practices en route, determined that, as with his own health problems, it was not practical or desirable to leave everything to the whims of nature.

Ironically, given this secular approach to the subject, it was in church that Tull had found his inspiration. He was looking at the church organ pipes with their holes and stops, and realised that this was the way forward with seed drills: boxes of seed with several drilled pipes, through which the grains were delivered when the device was pulled.

In spite of these quiet agricultural revolutions, life for the farm labourer went on as it had done for centuries. There was still plenty of work to be had for the experienced farmhand, and hiring fairs were the place where many found employment. Robert Plot, writing in 1677, gives a vivid illustration of this tradition:

> In the Northern part of Oxfordshire about Banbury and Bloxham, it has always been the custom at set times of the year for young people to meet to be hired as servants; which meeting, at Banbury they call the Mop; at Bloxham the Statute, where they all sort themselves, and carry their badges according as they are qualified; the carters standing in one place with their whips, and the shepherds in another with their crooks; but the maids, as far as I could observe, stood promiscuously; which custom I had scarce I think noted, but that it seems to be as old as our Saviour, and to illustrate His parable in St. Matthew's Gospel, where the Labourers are said to stand in the Market to be hired.

WITNEY : EARLY SUCCESS

Sheep farming was Oxfordshire's main source of income, with much of the money made in Witney. Writing in 1677, Robert Plot recorded:

> 'Tis certain that the blanketing trade of Witney is advanced to that height, that no place comes near it ... they owe it to a peculiar way of loose spinning the people have hereabout ... 'tis plain they are esteemed so far beyond all others, that this place has engrossed the whole trade of the nation for this commodity ... There are at least threescore in this town, that amongst them have at least 150 looms, employing 3000 poor people, from children of eight years old, to decrepit old age, do work out above a hundred packs of wool per week.

Plot also mentions Bampton as having a brisk trade in sheepskin 'jackets, breeches, leather-linings, etc ... no town in England having a trade like it in that sort of ware'. In the same breath he picks out the other foremost trades of the time – Oxford and Henley for malt, Burford for saddles, and Oxford again for gloves, knives and starch. These are humble reminders that in Oxford most people still depended on trades for their livelihood, as in any other city. Gloves, for example, had been an important trade there since the thirteenth century.

But it was Witney that dominated the cloth trade. Some men grew rich on the profits, including one John Holloway, who was able to siphon off some of his fortune to build six almshouses in the town for six poor blanket-weavers' widows. Likewise Henry Cornish, who built eight at Chipping Norton.

Thomas Early was one of a delegation who presented a pair of gold-fringed blankets to King James II when he visited Witney in 1688. Making his fortune in blankets, Early (along with the aforementioned John Holloway) was a founder, and master, of the Blue Coat School in Witney, for boys whose families worked in the local cloth-making industry. By the late 1830s, Early's descendants owned four of the six biggest blanket-weaving businesses in the town.

The Company of Blanket Weavers was formed in Witney in 1711, consolidating an industry that remained the area's chief source of income throughout the forthcoming Georgian era.

Banbury had its share of the cloth trade, too, with Cobb's factory opening in 1700, producing horsecloth and other woven materials. It was a relatively small business, but was able to thrive due to Banbury's position at the meeting of several trading routes. The factory eventually closed in the 1870s, with the coming of the railway. Banbury and Adderbury also had a busy production line of a worsted material called shag or plush. This industry went into terminal decline with the rise of factories in Coventry in the 1850s.

WOOD FELLED

In November 1695 a man called Wylde stumbled upon the 63-year-old Anthony Wood wielding pick and shovel in Merton Chapel. The historian explained that he was digging his own grave. He was ill, and suspected that he did not have long to live. He was keen to make sure that his final resting place should have the correct dimensions, and be in exactly the right place, 'close to the wall, next to the north door'. That is, indeed, where the ground-breaking historian is buried.

STUARTS STONED

Charles II's brother, James II, who was forced to abdicate in 1688, used Oxford as his base, from which he hoped to encourage a resurgent Catholicism in the land. University College was used for the celebration of Roman Catholic Mass, and the king caused a minor uprising when he installed a Catholic head at Magdalen College in 1687. He also interfered with the city's council, announcing that he was replacing twenty-eight members with men of his own choosing. These attempts to turn back the religious and administrative clocks were doomed to failure, but Oxford still retained Stuart/Jacobite sympathies after the demise of the last Stuart monarch Queen Anne in 1714.

When King William III (husband of penultimate Stuart monarch Mary II) visited Oxford in 1695, the Sheldonian Theatre prepared a grand feast. The monarch, however, believed that Jacobite plotters were attempting to poison him, and boycotted the party.

The Stuarts' close association with Oxford is captured in stone. Pembroke College has a statue of King James I on the side of the Hall. Charles I and Charles II can be seen lording it over the Botanical Gardens, in twin statues on the gateway, designed by Inigo Jones. Queens Mary II (1662–94) and Anne (1665–1714) gaze onto the High Street from the front of University College. Queen Anne also turns up in Tom Quad at Christ Church.

Most traces of the deposed Catholic king James II were removed from the island. The surviving statue on the interior side of the High Street-facing western gateway (the one with Anne on the street side) at University College is therefore a great rarity.

BLENHEIM PALACE: SPOILS OF WAR SPOILT

Blenheim Palace in the parish of Bladon was founded by John Churchill, 1st Duke of Marlborough, in 1705 and completed in 1724, a gift 'from the nation' for his pre-eminent role in securing victory in Bavaria at the Battle of Blenheim in 1704, a turning point in the War of the Spanish Succession. Thirty thousand French troops died at Blenheim, and the seemingly inexorable advance of a Roman Empire-style French Europe was effectively halted on that day. Marlborough went on to lead other famous victories at Ramillies in 1706, Oudenarde in 1708 and Malplaquet in 1709, by which time he was national hero bar none.

Queen Anne was a close friend to Sarah, the Duchess of Marlborough, but the 'gift from the nation' became increasingly grudging when the two women fell out. Their last clash occurred in 1711, after which Anne successfully petitioned Parliament to cancel the Blenheim funds.

Things had never run smoothly on the enormous building site (where the ruins of Woodstock Palace had been swept away on the whim of the duchess). The duke ignored the credentials of Christopher Wren, and opted instead for the playwright John Vanbrugh, an untrained architect who had recently worked with Nicholas Hawksmoor on Harewood House in Yorkshire. Going solo, Vanbrugh's designs were criticised from the outset, and were still being moaned about sixty years later. Writing in 1771, Arthur Young, passing through during an agricultural survey of the south of England, wrote:

> The front is a clutter of parts, so distinct, that a Gothic church has as
> much unity; and, withal, a heaviness in each part which is infinitely

disgusting ... Blenheim, upon the whole, can answer to none, who know it to be the monument of a nation's gratitude: a pile raised at the expense of the public, and meant to be great and magnificent, yet every thing that the occasion called for, might, and would have been effected, had not the execution fell to such a miserable architect as Vanbrugh, whose buildings are monuments of the vilest taste.

Gateway at Blenheim Palace.

With their money dried up, the royals disowning them, and the whole project turning into a white elephant, the Marlboroughs were forced into exile in 1714, owing the builders a huge sum. It was the year the War of the Spanish Succession finished, ironically, and Marlborough's star should have been at its zenith.

When Queen Anne died in 1714 and George I was installed, the Marlboroughs were back in favour. Vanbrugh was sacked, and Hawksmoor finished Blenheim, the construction of which was now financed entirely by the duke. In 1725 Vanbrugh visited the incomplete palace as a member of the public, but was turned away at the gate.

The builders finally cleared their gear away in the early 1730s. The 2,000 acres of finishing touches were added between 1763 and 1773 by Lancelot 'Capability' Brown, for the 4th Duke of Marlborough.

8

JACOBITES AND GEORGIANS
1714–1837

Like most other spans of time, the era of the Hanoverian kings was defined largely by war. It began with Blenheim Palace, built as a result of British success in the War of the Spanish Succession, soon to be replaced, in the 1740s, by the War of the Austrian Succession; and then the Seven Years War against France in the 1750s and '60s. The Jacobite uprisings, reverberating through pro-Stuart Oxford, and the loss of the American colonies, presided over by old Oxonian prime minister Frederick, Lord North, all left their mark, and the era was punctuated towards its end by the economic and social fallout of the Napoleonic Wars.

Much of Oxfordshire, notably the city of Oxford itself, retains a Georgian flavour in architectural terms. Many older buildings sport eighteenth-century facades, and new icons such as the Clarendon Building and Holywell Music Rooms were erected at this time. The Covered Market and the frontage of Queen's College are prominent monuments to the era. The latter has a statue of George II's queen, Caroline, decorating its roof. This would not be particularly noteworthy had Oxfordshire not been so vehemently anti-Hanoverian in the first half of the century.

Bull-baiting remained a popular national sport prior to the 1830s, and Oxfordshire was a keen player. Animals were tethered and baited with dogs at the Bull Ring in the middle of Oxford near the busy crossroads of Carfax. Bulls were also baited at Headington and other neighbouring villages, nearby Wheatley being so keen that its bouts continued until the sport's final suppression in 1832 – one of the last surviving bull-baits in England.

Victorian-era prime minister William Gladstone, recalling his time at Christ Church in the 1830s, claimed that the college's chief pastimes were rat-killing, cock-fighting, otter-hunting and badger-baiting. A vicar at Wheatley spent much ink and passion deploring the latter sport and imploring his parishioners to desist. It would take the anti-cruelty-to-animals-inspired legislation of the 1820s and '30s to finally let the badger out of the bag, and allow the county's bull rings to quietly rust.

GEORGE I AND THE OLD PRETENDER

In 1714 Queen Anne, last of the Stuart monarchs, died, without any surviving children. The other members of the Stuart family were too steeped in Catholicism to gain favour with the Protestant English establishment, and so in came the tenuously related Hanoverians.

The 1701 Act of Settlement had been a Protestant get-out clause redirecting the royal line to Sophia of the Palatinate, aka Sophia of Hanover, granddaughter of James I of England, in the event of William III or Queen

Anne dying childless. This is how, when both Sophia and Anne died in 1714, the heir was Sophia's son George, Anne's second cousin. There were over fifty surviving Stuart heirs with closer blood ties to the throne.

Oxford was not happy with this succession and acquired the nickname 'the Jacobite Capital of England'. The university had always favoured the Stuarts, combining this with a staunch support of the Church of England. Oxford undergraduates had marked the death of Queen Mary with celebrations, sensing that the royal line would have to veer back to James II's son James Francis Edward – soon to be styled 'the Old Pretender'. In pro-Catholic Thame the authorities were equally unhappy with the prospect of a German Protestant on the throne.

The simmer only began to boil over when the Old Pretender wrote to the university in 1715, claiming that the new Hanoverian establishment planned to undermine its powers and seize university land. When the city officially celebrated George I's birthday on 28 May that year, the first riots erupted. Malcontents, numbering thousands according to some pro-Jacobite reports, converged outside The King's Head Tavern on the High Street, favourite watering hole of pro-establishment Whigs. Stones were thrown, one man receiving a deep head wound, and the town's celebratory Georgian bonfire was dismantled, opportunistic protesters smuggling away most of the faggots for their own hearths.

The mob was soon reinforced by drinkers from neighbouring pubs, and the Whigs had to flee through a back entrance. College proctors – the university police – managed to restore some degree of order; but the whole thing flared up again later when a Whig from Oriel College, bastion of establishment support, fired his gun and injured a Brasenose student. Any window sporting a candle – a mark of loyalty to George on his birthday – was stoned. Turning their attentions from the successfully holed-up Whigs, the rioters attacked a Presbyterian meeting house in St Ebbes, using the makeshift chapel's furniture to construct their own bonfire, mocking the official fires of the birthday celebrations.

Presbyterian minister William Roby, staunch supporter of the Hanoverian succession, was put in the town stocks, and his effigy was burnt, Guy Fawkes-style. Town constables were too few in number to disperse the crowds.

Things were even more fevered on the following day, 29 May, anniversary of the restoration of Stuart king Charles II. It was very unfortunate timing, having George's birthday back-to-back with this auspicious date. Oxford celebrated as if the Restoration were happening all over again, students wearing sprigs of oak in their hats and lighting so many bonfires that authorities feared the city would be burnt down. People ran through the streets shouting 'King James III! The true king! No usurper!' Oriel College was stoned and several people were injured, and Baptist and Presbyterian meeting places were vandalised.

The clergy's official line was to condemn the Jacobites, and in spite of strong support for the revolt in 1715 in much of Oxfordshire, and an unofficial stocktaking of the available men, horses and arms who could support the Duke of Ormond (who was expected to lead the Jacobite cause in the south), order was eventually maintained in the county.

Fears of a Jacobite takeover lingered for many months, however. A consignment of smuggled arms – 140 swords and 244 bayonets – was intercepted in Oxford in

October 1715, and dragoons later arrested suspected ringleaders. The mayor spoke of 'pestilent fellows who fomented sedition', even as open chants supporting 'James III' and Ormond were heard from gangs promenading the streets. But the feared rebellion effectively came to an end when three chief Oxford conspirators, Gordon, Kerr and Dorwell, were sentenced to death and hanged at Tyburn in London on 7 December 1715. New bouts of pro-Jacobite violence coloured the first half of 1716, but failed to rekindle the flame.

GEORGE II AND THE YOUNG PRETENDER

The Jacobite cause peaked during the reign of George II (1727-1760). The rebellion of 'Young Pretender' Charles Edward Stuart, grandson of James II, made it as far south as Derby in 1745, before retreating back to Scotland where the uprising met its nemesis at the Battle of Culloden in April 1746. But even after this there were many people who wanted to oust the Hanoverians; and Oxford folklore maintains that two Jacobite students were hanged under Magdalen Bridge in 1745 for belonging to the pro-pretender White Rose Club.

In February 1748 pro-pretender students took to the streets of Oxford again; but by now such sympathies were very much underground rather than mainstream. In April the university formally condemned the students involved, making 'a public declaration of our sincere abhorrence and detestation of such factions and seditious practices, as also of our firm resolution to punish offenders (of what state or quality soever they are) who shall duly be convicted thereof, according to the uttermost severity and rigour of our statutes'. The 'soever they are' note was a warning that offenders would not be able to hide behind titles and peerages.

Several of the ringleaders – 'beardless striplings of sedition', according to the summary in *The Newgate Calendar*, one of the most popular books of the nineteenth century – were apprehended. Two students, John Whitmore and Jeremiah Dawes, were found guilty, fined, and imprisoned for two years.

The year 1748 was to be the last of noteworthy Jacobitism in Oxfordshire. The city of Oxford had now entrenched its loyalist position, and any lingering support for the cause was reduced to a philosophical and sentimental level, the chief expression of which was the university's officially outlawed (and therefore highly attractive) White Rose Club. New member Evelyn Waugh wrote in 1923: 'I also joined the White Rose Club, an occasional dining club devoted to the Stuart cause.'

OXFORD MPS: ANOTHER GREAT DAY FOR DEMOCRACY

MP Thomas Rowney was happy to lay on lavish feasts for the Oxford electorate – consisting of around 3,000 landowning men – as part of the unspoken deal by which they would re-elect him. On one such occasion, the men drank far too much and proceeded to stagger around the town throwing stones through windows. They came to Rowney's house and hooted drunkenly. Rowney gamely came outside and hooted along with them.

Thomas Rowney stepped down in 1759, ending a family reign that had begun with his own father in 1695.

Nine years later the local council in Oxford, under mayor Isaac Lawrence, made an appeal to his successors. If Oxford's two MPs would agree to pay off the city's debts, they said, the council would return them to Parliament unopposed at the next election. The MPs were warned that if they refused, 'the whole council are determined to apply to some other person in the county to do it, and if possible, by that means to keep themselves from being sold to foreigners'.

The MPs were outraged by this odd form of blackmail-cum-bribery, and reported the mayor and councillors of Oxford to the House of Commons, as a result of which Lawrence and the ten members of the council were sent to Newgate Prison. Reprimanded and pardoned four days later, the mayor appealed to George Spencer, 4th Duke of Marlborough, to pay off the debts, and he duly transferred £6,000 – more than half a million in today's money – into the city's piggybank, on condition that he could select a candidate for Parliament. The duke's man – his younger brother, Lord Robert Spencer – was duly elected in 1768.

The city's second MP at this time was 25-year-old William Harcourt, 3rd Earl Harcourt, who spent most of his life as a field marshal and court official to George III. He took part in the expedition to Havana during the Seven Years War, and commanded troops during the American Revolution and the Flanders Campaign of the French Revolutionary Wars. He ended his career as governor of the Royal Military College at Great Marlow in Buckinghamshire, dying in June 1830, and was interred back where he started: at Stanton Harcourt. In all, he had little time for his duties as an Oxford MP.

Party lines were first drawn in the 1754 elections, in which Oxfordshire was split between what were called the Old Interest and New Interest. The Old supported the Jacobite cause, in spite of the catastrophe of the Battle of Culloden in 1745, while the New were staunch defenders of the Hanoverians. The latter were referred to as Whigs (although the first Oxford MP to formally declare party affiliation was the Whig James Langston in 1826). In the 1754 election, the Old faction won most votes, but the House of Commons overruled the result and elected the aforementioned Thomas Rowney and Robert Lee, 4th Earl of Lichfield (who died after falling from his horse during a hunt in 1776).

By the end of the eighteenth century the Woodstock constituency had just 200 voters, and the MP was simply chosen by the Duke of Marlborough from the very undemocratic confines of Blenheim Palace. This was what was known as a 'pocket borough', a variant of the rotten borough. Likewise, in Banbury, the North family of Wroxton Abbey pulled the strings at every election. Their most famous incumbent was Frederick, Lord North, MP between 1754 and 1790, and prime minister between 1770 and 1780. History remembers him as the man who lost America – the revolution there was fought and lost during his tenure.

By the reign of George III, Jacobite passions were all spent. The mood swung completely the other way, so much so that in 1829 when Oxford University's MP Robert Peel supported the Bill for Catholic Emancipation, opposition was so strong that he called a by-election, and failed to regain his seat. He was elected soon afterwards to the rotten borough of Westbury in Wiltshire.

Oxford remained opposed to all forms of reform and emancipation, setting it in sharp contrast to the progressive

politicians of Banbury. The latter were active supporters of
the Reform Act which became law in 1832, celebrating its
extension of suffrage (so that one in five men could now
vote), its removal of rotten boroughs, and its reduction of
aristocratic power. The man elected by Banbury that year,
Henry Tancred, a Whig, was the MP until 1859.

Not that reform brought an end to political corrup-
tion. In Oxford in 1832 it was still traditional for the
town clerk to issue beer tokens to electors, to ensure
their support at the ballot box. All the men had to do
then was stagger through a narrow doorway at the Town
Hall, and that counted as a vote.

The Municipal Reform Act of 1835 cleared up some
of these charming but farcical anomalies. It also established free trade, the final nail in the coffin for trade
monopolies that dated back to the medieval guilds. The
Act also had a loophole for the university: '... nothing
in the Act contained shall be construed to alter or affect
the Rights and Privileges Duties of Liabilities, of The
University of Oxford'.

THE WESLEY METHOD

Methodist pioneers and brothers John and Charles
Wesley were Oxford men. John had studied at Christ
Church, was elected a fellow of Lincoln College in
1726, and became an Anglican priest two years later.
Charles, too, was educated at Christ Church, and was
ordained there, taking Anglican orders in 1735. Charles
formed a prayer group for Oxford students in 1727,
with John joining and becoming its spiritual leader in
1729. Members of the group were heckled and ridiculed

by other students, and dubbed the 'Holy Club' or 'the Methodists', on account of their methodical and pedantically detailed Bible study and lifestyle.

In spite of being Anglican priests, and – initially at least – encouraging their 'Methodist' followers to attend the local church, the clergy and university opposed them. With many churches banning them from entering, the Methodists had little option other than to open churches of their own. In the late 1730s a Methodist congregation of 1,200 in Burford was nothing unusual. John Wesley praised the attentiveness of the people there, and at Witney too.

The Wesleys were busy in Oxford in the 1730s, opening a Sunday school for poor children, and visiting the city's prisoners and invalids. The chief audience for Methodism came from the poorer end of society. It was a social diocese which the Wesleys embraced, but not one they always enjoyed. In Henley John Wesley described 'a wild staring congregation, many of them void both of common sense and common decency'. He claims to have reprimanded them for this, and noted a slight improvement on his return visit in 1768. He wrote that 'one or two of the baser sort made some noise, but I reproved them, and, for once, they were ashamed'.

John Wesley visited Thame to preach Methodism in the 1780s. His congregation met on the top floor of a cottage on a site now occupied by Coral's bookmakers (which John would most certainly not have approved of). The numbers were so great that the floor collapsed, spilling the congregation into the room below. It was a powerful symbol of the downward direction they might take in the afterlife, but it also brought home to the Wesleys the need for sound, purpose-built Methodist churches.

LONG-DISTANCE TRANSPORTATION

In the early nineteenth century, the British colonies in Australia were in need of old-fashioned slave labour, much to the relief of the overcrowded prisons. At the Oxford Assizes the justices did their best to feed demand by sending as many men overseas as possible. As a snapshot of this trend, the following unfortunates were listed in *Jackson's Oxford Journal*, 8 March 1828:

> William Bolton, 25, charged with receiving stolen property – 14 years' transportation. James Lamb, 25, for stealing £12 19s 6d from the person of Rich. Henderson, at Cropredy – fourteen years' transportation. Edward Morris, 40, for stealing a pair of breeches, the property of John Allsop, of Wheatley – fourteen years' transportation. Richard Huck, 21, charged with breaking into a dwelling house ... at Fulbrook ... and stealing six £1 notes and a crown piece, seven years' transportation. James Hemmings, 21, charged with feloniously stealing from ... John Salmon, of Hardwick, a quantity of wearing apparel, his property – seven years' transportation. William Cranfield, 38, charged with stealing ... at Shiplake, a silver watch and two gold seals, value £5 – seven years' transportation. Eliza Stow, 15, charged with breaking open the dwelling house of James Savery, of Chadlington, and stealing a coral necklace, a net cap, a thimble case, &c. – seven years' transportation.

Relatively petty thefts such as these were the deeds that fed the colonies' needs. Bigger hauls, such as Charles Langford's £50 theft, reported at the same assize, still brought the death penalty, as did sheep stealing. These harsh penalties were toned down considerably in the wave of reform that swept in during the 1830s.

Gamekeepers managed to collar many a potential transportee, and the deer parks of Shotover and Wychwood provided dozens of them. The Oxfordshire Sessions heard endless pleas, including a 1788 case where commoner Thomas James was gaoled for 'cruelly beating three Wychwood game keepers'. In 1824 assistant gamekeeper James Millin was murdered, and suspects were swiftly, possibly arbitrarily, rounded up. In 1836 Edmund Harding and William Stafford were transported to Australia for seven years after being found guilty of assaulting a keeper.

THE SPIRIT OF MACHEATH

Reigning briefly as the county's most infamous highwayman, Isaac Darkin, aka Dumas the Highwayman, was arrested after a robbery near Nettlebed. Throughout his trial and on the gallows he showed great disdain and bravado, much to the delight of the crowd and the dismay of his female admirers, whose numbers had reached fanclub proportions. He was executed on 23 March 1761, and the event was reported widely:

This morning was executed in Oxford the noted Darkin, alias Dumas, for robbing Mr. Gamon on the highway. His behaviour was extremely undaunted; for when he came out of the gaol to the ladder, he ascended it with the greatest resolution ... he put the cord round his own neck ... pulled out a white handkerchief, tied it round his eyes and face, and went off without saying a word. His body was ordered to be brought back into the castle, to be conveyed to the Museum for dissection; but he declaring that he valued not death, but only the thoughts of being anatomized, a large gang of

bargemen arose, took him away in triumph, carried him to the next
parish church; and while some rung bells for joy, others opened
his belly, filled it with unslack'd lime, and then buried the body.
(From the London newspaper *Public Ledger or The Daily Register
of Commerce and Intelligence*, 25 March 1761)

Dumas's intention in leaping from the gallows had been
to emulate his hero, the fictional, unrepentant Captain
Macheath from John Gay's hugely popular *The Beggar's
Opera* (1728).

Giles Covington, a 21-year-old seaman and petty
criminal, was arrested for the murder of a pedlar at
Abingdon. Richard Kilby, an army deserter suspected
of the crime, pointed the finger at Giles and an accom-
plice, Charles Shury, in order to gain a royal pardon.
Covington protested his innocence throughout the trial,
writing contrite pleading letters from Oxford Prison. But
the verdict was not overturned.

A large crowd turned out on 7 March 1791 at Oxford
Castle to see Covington die. Before he took the plunge,
wearing his sailor's uniform complete with white gloves
and white hatband, he tossed a letter in the air, asking
that it should be read out. But he didn't hang around
to see his request carried out, jumping to his death as
soon as the noose was round his neck – another nod to
Macheath from *The Beggar's Opera*.

Like Shury before him, Covington was cut down and
delivered to Dr Christopher Pegge at Christ Church
College for the Anatomy School. His bones were later
wired together, and the skeleton of Giles Covington
became a teaching aid. In 1860 the bones were displayed
in the new University Museum of Natural History on
Parks Road. It stood here in a glass case well into the

1960s, with a label reading simply 'Englishman'. It was on display in the Museum of Oxford until 2010, and in spite of ongoing attempts to have the remains buried, and to have the man's name cleared by royal pardon, Giles is still hanging in store to this day.

Giles Covington and his comrades were not alone in being picked to pieces after death. Prior to the Anatomy Act of 1832 it was common practice for judges to condemn victims to the gallows first and the dissection table afterwards. Even the ones who were allowed a gentler decay in the graveyard were often dug up by body-snatchers to feed the demand for teaching-aid corpses.

In 2000 an archaeological dig at the Old Ashmolean building in Oxford – currently home to the Museum of the History of Science – shed a little light on what was being handed over to the Anatomy School in the nineteenth century. In all, 2,050 human bones were unearthed, belonging to between fifteen and thirty individuals buried during the seventeenth and eighteenth centuries. They were mainly adult males – not surprising given the usual victims of the gallows – but also included three foetuses, an adolescent boy and two women. The skulls of the adults had been sawn in half, indicating that the brain had been removed for pickling.

In addition, there were 900 animal bones, the most unusual being the fore-limb of a manatee.

THE ROCKY ROAD TO OXFORDSHIRE

In the mid-sixteenth century the journey from Oxford to London took around sixteen hours, depending on the time of year and the corresponding state of the

London road. On bad days, you couldn't even get into Headington. By the Restoration the journey had been reduced to thirteen hours, in dry conditions, with the arrival of 'fly coach' fast services. However, increased coach traffic made the roads deteriorate even further, and for passengers travel was a grim ordeal.

Turnpike Trusts were the partial answer to the problem, with toll gates built at various points, the proceeds from which went towards surfacing and maintaining the roads. Some of the toll houses still stand in Oxford, Witney, Dorchester and elsewhere. The first of these trusts in Oxfordshire was set up to cover the stretch of London road between Oxford and Stokenchurch. The road from Burford to Northleach in Gloucestershire was turnpiked in 1751, as was the Oxford to Witney road (and the toll booth between Eynsham and Oxford is still in operation, although as a private business rather than a means of repairing the roads).

The Swinford ferry was replaced with a bridge in 1777. By the end of the century all the major roads in Oxfordshire had been turnpiked. It was an improvement – but all things are relative. Arthur Young, travelling in 1769, complained:

> The road from Witney to Northleach is, I think, the worst turnpike I ever travelled in, so bad that it is a scandal to the country. They mend and make with nothing but the stone which forms the under stratum ... by using it alone, in pieces as large as one's head, the road is rendered most execrable. I travelled it with a very low opinion of all the counties and places it leads to; for if they were inhabited by people of fortune and spirit, I should think they would never suffer such a barbarous method of mending their capital road to subsist.

By the 1820s the roads were in a decent state at last, and Oxford received over seventy coaches a day, while Banbury welcomed more than fifty, both settlements becoming major coaching centres, and Bicester, Burford and Chipping Norton very much on the road map too.

It was the golden age before the decline, with rail becoming the dominant means of travel as the Victorian era advanced. The Great Western Railway opened a station near Folly Bridge in 1814, and had linked Oxford to London by 1837. With the arrival of other rail lines in the city, and stations at Steventon, Didcot, Botley, Banbury and elsewhere, the long reign (and reins) of the horse-drawn coach was finally at an end. The last Turnpike Trusts were closed down in the 1870s.

MESSING ABOUT WITH THE RIVER

While people travelled by road – and then train – the big revolution in cargo transport was on the new canal network in the eighteenth century. In Oxford, the canals, with water levels that could be controlled, solved another problem faced by boatmen using the Thames – the drying up of the river. As seventeenth-century historian Robert Plot wrote: 'The River Thames is not made so perfectly navigable to Oxford, but that in dry times, barges do sometimes lie aground three weeks, or a month, or more.'

In Plot's day, goods shipped from London to Oxford via the Thames had to stop at Burcot. The river was unnavigable beyond the village, and the barges had to unload their cargoes onto wagons for the rest of the journey. In 1635 a barge made it through to Oxford for the first time.

In times past, water millers had been known to dam the rivers, and landowners to install locks, so that they could charge fees for the passage of river traffic. Various Acts of Parliament tried to improve Thames traffic, but progress was slow. In 1714 it was reported that pedestrians could cross some areas of the Thames in Oxfordshire without getting their feet wet. Even when there was water, it could take up to eight weeks to take a barge from Oxford to London.

The Oxford Canal was constructed to link London to the industrial Midlands. The Coventry to Banbury stretch was finished in 1774, and the final stretch to Oxford was completed in 1790. The main boat yard on the canal was the site now known as Tooley's Boatyard in Banbury. For all its ingenious beauty, much of the canal was built as cheaply as possible: single gates on the locks instead of double ones, lift or swing-bridges instead of sturdier, more expensive brick ones, the use of the existing stretches of the River Cherwell, and constructing twists and turns to get round hills (a so-called 'contour canal') rather than getting engineers to employ tunnels or aqueducts. Some of these contours were ironed out in the 1820s, but many remain.

One of the most important cargoes delivered by barge was coal. Some areas of Oxfordshire had a severe wood shortage, due to so much forest having been felled during the English Civil Wars. In Upper and Lower Heyford, for example, people were burning straw, rags, dung and turf, in the absence of any other fuel. The realisation that canals would almost halve the price of coal – previously shipped by sea and river from faraway Newcastle-upon-Tyne – was one of the most important impetuses behind the new waterways. The Oxford Canal had several wharves along its length for unloading coal, including ones at the previously fuel-starved villages of Heyford, Cropredy and Souldern.

The Oxford Canal's heyday was brief, though. Between 1790 and 1805 it carried all water traffic between London and the Midlands, but then the Grand Junction Canal opened, and much of the London traffic chose this new, more direct route. The one section that remained busy was between Napton and Braunston, which formed a link between the Warwick and Napton Canal and the Grand Junction. The Oxford Canal Company had opposed the new canal, of course, and the Act which allowed the competition to go ahead included a clause by which Grand Junction paid Oxford 'bar tolls' as a form of compensation for the loss of traffic.

Canal at Lower Heyford.

Always a bit old fashioned, horses were used on the Oxford Canal long after animal brawn had been superseded by coal and diesel. The last beast-powered barge retired in 1959. It had been pulled by a mule and was the last of Britain's horse-drawn freight narrowboats.

TAKING A FENCE AT OTMOOR

The fencing off of common land in England was enacted through a series of Enclosure Acts. The earliest of these had been in 1604 (and the last was in 1914), but Oxfordshire had experienced the issue even earlier. A 1517 report showed how landowners had already staked their claim, illegally, to over 8,500 acres of arable Oxfordshire. Most of this had been converted to sheep and cattle pasture – the main aim of enclosure – and several hundred people had been evicted as a result. Records note that evicted families from Binsey 'led an evil and wretched existence until life ended', and those booted off the land in Little Rollright by the abbot of Eynsham Abbey wept as they went.

The so-called Oxford Rising of 1596 had objected to these unhindered land-grabs. But in the eighteenth century the trend became more of a free-for-all, and once large-scale enclosure was under way it was like a downhill race without brakes.

Common land, often called wasteland, had never been owned by commoners as such, but by the local lord of the manor. Commoners did have certain rights on this land, however, such as grazing or wood-collecting. In Oxfordshire it is not difficult to appreciate how this looked in practice, as two large areas of unenclosed medieval common have survived on the edges of Oxford, at Port Meadow and Wolvercote.

In 1815 an Enclosure Act allowed Lord Abingdon to enclose and drain Otmoor. In 1829 this led to rioting, in an alliance of commoners, farmers and tradesmen. The men with rights to the common were all told they could take a share of the moor as long as they paid towards the drainage and enclosure; but, of course, not many could afford to do so.

Lord Abingdon, and other landowners who were allowed to buy the commoners' lots for £5 each, had been handed a legal right to land that had been used by villagers from several surrounding villages – Beckley, Charlton-on-Otmoor, Fencott, Horton-cum-Studley, Murcott, Noke and Oddington – 'since time immemorial'. Morally, the commoners had a strong argument, but in the absence of any legal documents granting common rights, legally they had no case. However, resistance was so strong that the protest was dubbed 'the Otmoor Revolution' by the local press, and many landowners were ready to capitulate, waiving their newfound rights in order to maintain the peace.

Local men, with their faces blacked to hide their identities, uprooted fences and hedges and patrolled Otmoor with guns and farming implements. But Lord Abingdon dug in his heels, and by 1834 the fight had gone from the revolution.

Wychwood Forest was largely cleared and enclosed in the 1850s and '60s, partly on the pretext that it was the haunt of poachers and other criminals. The owner of Cornbury Park received 1,500 acres of the enclosed forest in 1862, and ironically this is all that remains of Wychwood Forest, which had once covered 102,400 acres.

BLANKET COVERAGE IN WITNEY

By the beginning of Queen Victoria's reign, Witney firm John Early's was the biggest blanket-weaving business in the county, employing seventy people. The Earlys had been in the trade for 100 years, and were at the forefront of innovations. They introduced fly shuttles in 1800 and power looms in 1852 (but they succumbed to economic hardship at last, closing down in 2002). This was the final shift of the spinning and weaving trade away from its cottage industry origins to the intensive production lines of mills and factories. These were centred in and around Witney, employing around 800 by the time the power looms arrived.

Witney blankets did not have one specific style, but they were renowned for their thick, weatherproof 'pile'. In 1716 playwright and poet John Gay summed this up in his poem *Trivia*:

> *True Witney Broad-cloth with its Shag unshorn,*
> *Unpierc'd is in the lashing Tempest worn.*

Another Georgian success story was Bliss's Mill at Chipping Norton, established in 1746. It specialised in horse blankets and other material associated with the busy Oxford to Worcester coach traffic that passed through the town. In the early 1800s it switched to tweed and serge, for which it gained an international reputation. Its last incarnation opened in 1870, and was in business until 1980.

Some of the people working in the cloth trade were the inhabitants of a long-established but now rapidly expanding institution – the workhouse. In Banbury, for example, the workhouse supplied a man called Richard Burrowes with up to fifty paupers to work in the manufacture of worsted, for a pittance, food and clothing. The workforce were aged between 8 and 60. Another man, Thomas Wilkes of Wiggington, employed the local poor, on condition that he provided clothes for them, and nursed and/or buried them when their time came.

This kind of practice was in the interests of the local authorities and workhouses, as it took responsibility for poor folk off their hands, just as charities and foodbanks do today. It was a simple case of auctioning off the poor to the highest bidder.

NAPOLEONIC WARS: WINNERS AND LOSERS

To put the poverty of the early nineteenth century into perspective, by 1803 one fifth of the inhabitants of Oxfordshire were claiming aid or alms of some kind. It was a combination of many things – the enclosure of the land, which took away most of the commons that had provided grazing, growing and gathering; the mechanisation of farming, which brought an end to many jobs; population growth; the anachronistic Settlement Laws, dating from 1662, which tied people to their place of birth, and which were not repealed until 1834; and the general poverty brought about by the Napoleonic Wars, which had begun to empty the coffers nationwide in May 1803, and would last another twelve years.

Patrick Moulder, landlord of the Cross Keys pub in Witney, was one of hundreds of Oxfordshire men who fought in the Napoleonic Wars. A soldier in the 15th Hussars, he took part in the battles of Corunna, Vitoria, the Pyrenees, Orthes, Toulouse and Waterloo. He finished as RSM of the Oxfordshire Yeomanry Cavalry; but his war experiences had taken a toll. In December 1838 he blew his own brains out. The inquest heard how his servant discovered him with 'his head shot to atoms'. Regardless of this ignominious end, Moulder was buried at Witney parish church later that year with full military honours, and over 3,000 came to pay their respects.

The year 1815 brought victory for Britain, and the final defeat of Napoleon Bonaparte. But for thousands of soldiers returning to their homes in Oxfordshire, there was no work. The workhouses boomed with this sad harvest.

In 1834, the system of poor relief was reformed. The task of looking after the poor was removed from individual parishes, and Oxfordshire was divided into eight Poor Law Unions, each with a Board of Guardians made up of representatives from the parishes. New Union Workhouses were the chief weapon in the poverty war. There were just eight of these in the county, at Banbury, Bicester, Chipping Norton, Headington, Henley, Thame, Witney and Woodstock, with another opening on Oxford's Cowley Road in 1865.

It is still often claimed that Abingdon Gaol was built by prisoners of the Napoleonic Wars in 1811. There is no evidence for this, however, and there were no French prisoners in Abingdon or Oxfordshire at the time. It is more likely that prisoners from Oxford Prison were used.

Abingdon Gaol was ready for use in 1812, but in 1860 it was condemned as unfit for purpose, and in spite of attempts to raise money for renovation, it was closed down in 1868. It was used as a grain store for many years, and the main part of the building is still standing, converted into residential and commercial premises in 2011.

9

THE VICTORIAN AGE
1837–1901

Although medieval college foundations and Georgian facades on older buildings abound, many of the larger landmark buildings of Oxford were built in the nineteenth century – the Ashmolean, the Natural History/ Pitt Rivers complex, the Town Hall, the Randolph Hotel, the Oxford University Press on Walton Street, the Taylor Institution fronted by four statues modelled on four Oxford sisters called Ogle, and the subtly dragon-decorated Examination Schools. There were also several new colleges, and plenty of the neo-Gothic gloss that dominates churches throughout the island, from domineering renovations like St Mary Magdalen on Magdalen Street, to newbuilds such as St Frideswide's on Botley Road and St Ebbe's behind the Westgate Shopping Centre.

The great liberation of the navel-gazing, ineffectual and impractical university began with three Acts: the Sacramental Test Act of 1828, repealing the requirement for all government and university officials to belong to the Church of England; the Roman Catholic Relief Act of 1829; and the University Act of 1854, which made it possible for non-Church of England members to study at Oxford. By the 1870s modernity had swept in, sidelining denominational tussles, and (after 1875) generating waves of female students and academics – still in their own segregated schools and colleges, but able for the first time to take advantage of Oxford University resources.

The university now adopted the continental model of offering BA degrees based on separate schools (history, mathematics, literature, natural sciences, medicine, etc.), and shifted at last from the farcical five-minute oral examination to gruelling written exams, taken in the newly built Examination Schools.

Away from the University, the bulk of Oxfordshire's population remained poor, and there were many slum areas, notably St Ebbes, St Thomas' and St Clements in Oxford, and the 'Waterloo' district in Grimsbury, Banbury, which became a major residential suburb after constant redevelopment between 1881 and 1930.

The expansion of the railways opened Oxfordshire to the rest of the island in the Victorian era. The university had tried to block attempts to open railway stations in the city, but elsewhere the new mode of transport was unstoppable. And not without its mishaps, as is grimly illustrated by the Shipton-on-Cherwell disaster. A passenger train was derailed there on Christmas Eve 1874:

The Inquest on the victims of the terrible accident near Oxford was opened on Saturday in the Manor House of Hampton Gay, the residence of Mr Pearson, a paper manufacturer, who, with the whole of his employees, rendered admirable assistance to the maimed and wounded passengers immediately after the accident ... The coroner and jury then proceeded to view the twenty-six bodies, lying in the paper Mill close by ... The train was crowded with passengers, for the most part journeying to various parts to spend Christmas with their friends. It was somewhat late at Oxford, and after starting was, no doubt, travelling at a fair rate of speed, when, on nearing Hampton Gay Church, where the line crosses an embankment ... the tyre of one of the wheels of a carriage suddenly broke, and threw the vehicle off the rails ... all rolled over the embankment in a state of ruin ... In a moment after the crash the air was filled with the shrieks and screams of the wounded and dying ... Altogether it was a scene of horror indescribable ... At present there are thirty-one people lying dead at Oxford, and the injured and wounded are said to be upwards of seventy. (*Bradford Observer*, 28 December 1874)

EDUCATING OXFORDSHIRE

Ironically for a county centred on Oxford and its famous university, education was not one of the county's strong suits prior to the Victorian era. It had opened its share of grammar schools and then charity schools, but the coverage was very patchy, and the quality of education was very inconsistent. The nonconformist schools of the mid- to late-eighteenth century made some amends, as did various private schools, but it was not until the expansion of education and a more carefully rolled-out education policy in the nineteenth century that things took an upturn.

The initial driver behind this upsurge in education was the Church. Much of the teaching took place in Sunday schools. In schools that opened on other days, children had to miss lessons due to work commitments, and as late as the 1850s in Mixbury and Yarnton it was usual for children to finish school at the age of 8 or 9.

At their most basic, lessons were limited to learning passages of the Bible, but at least they involved a little reading. At its best it coalesced into Church-funded day schools. Those in Banbury and Charlbury were amongst the first, and these laid the foundations for the modern education system, which got under way with the Elementary Education Act 1870. This established School Boards in most places, although Banbury, already well organised, managed without one.

The bulk of the Oxfordshire population remained poor in the first half of the century. Lace-making employed thousands of women and children in the Bicester area during the nineteenth century. In 1859 a damning report on the industry concluded: 'All accounts agree in representing the occupation of lace-making in these districts as highly injurious to those engaged in it.'

Consumption and dyspepsia killed many lace-makers, mainly girls, some as young as 4. Stunted growth resulted from their cramped twelve-plus hour shifts, with no exercise or fresh air, and it was said you could tell a lace-maker from her walk. Other physical conditions noted were scrofula, indigestion, distortion of the spine, and poor eyesight sometimes leading to blindness. For older females, difficult labours, miscarriages and 'derangement of the uterine functions' were said to be 'almost universal'.

Shutford got its own power looms in 1885, surviving the shift of textile industries to the urban centres of the West Midlands and the North West by concentrating on niche-market, high-quality plush for liveries, upholstery and furnishings. Such was its reputation that Nicholas II, the last Tsar of Russia, ordered Shutford plush for his coronation in 1896, having encountered it during a visit to England shortly before his accession. Unfortunately for the tsar, the material was not bulletproof. He was executed in 1918. Shutford's plush industry died thirty years later.

UNIVERSITY CHALLENGES

Between 1334 and 1827, anyone working or studying at the university had to take the Stamford Oath. The gist was that you swore never to work in any university other than Oxford and Cambridge, and the practical outcome was that no new English universities were built. The origin of this was in 1333, when a group of students had absconded to Stamford in Lincolnshire (famously taking the Brasenose College brass doorknocker with them).

It had resulted in an extraordinary Oxbridge monopoly. While the rest of Europe (including Scotland) had been sprouting universities for 500 years, in 1827 England only had two. But the revoking of the Stamford Oath in that year opened the floodgates. The University of London (now University College London) opened its doors in 1828, and Durham University was founded in 1833 (having been thwarted in this ambition by Oxford in 1660). Oxford and Cambridge, although they vigorously opposed these first few foundations, were soon resigned to new universities across the land. This is symbolised most vividly with Balliol College's master Benjamin Jowett helping found Bristol University in 1876.

Revolutionary change was afoot elsewhere in the city, with the final triumph of Town over Gown in Oxford. The university had run the city since the time of the St Scholastica's Day riot in 1355. In 1771 the city and the university began to run the town together; but the 1836 Municipal Corporation Act was the reform that paved the way for fundamental change, including a rudimentary city police force, and a local Board of Health (established in 1865 and jointly populated by Town and

Gown). Similar reforms were introduced in Banbury at the same time too, and a county police force was established in 1857.

Oxford's Board of Health supervised such areas as paving, lighting, hygiene, flood control, fire brigade, tramways and general improvements. Finally, in 1889, the city corporation took on these roles itself, Oxford became a county borough, and the modern city was upon us.

HUXLEY AND WILBERFORCE: PLANET OF THE APES

When Charles Darwin first published his evolutionary theory, many men, including eminent biologist Thomas Huxley, kicked themselves for not getting there first. It was, said Huxley, one of those things which seems blindingly obvious once it has been explained, the evidence, in the form of farm animals, dog breeds, fancy pigeons, etc., having been there for centuries.

Not everyone was open to the implications of Darwin's work, though. A celebrated evolution-versus-creation debate took place in 1860, dominated by Thomas Huxley and Samuel Wilberforce, Bishop of Oxford. It was twelve months after the appearance of Darwin's *On the Origin of Species*, and Huxley (aka Darwin's Bulldog, the Richard Dawkins of his day) had visited the almost-completed Oxford University Museum of Natural History to attend a meeting of the British Association.

Huxley had intended leaving before the debate, but was goaded into taking part. Wilberforce expressed his dismay at the thought that 'a venerable ape' might be his ancestor, asking Huxley whether it was through his grandfather or grandmother that he claimed such descent. The vehement Huxley replied:

> If I am asked whether I would choose to be descended from the poor animal of low intelligence and stooping gait, who grins and chatters as we pass, or from a man, endowed with great ability and splendid position, who should use these gifts to discredit and crush humble seekers after truth, I hesitate what answer to make.

NEWMAN, OLD RELIGION

The rise of the Methodist Church and the various other dissenters' movements in the preceding two centuries had seemed an unstoppable force, especially as it appealed to the poor, who made up the vast majority of the British population. At the same time, laws against Catholicism had been slowly dismantled since 1766, with the Roman Catholic Relief Act 1829 finally removing many of the religious restrictions first laid down nearly 300 years earlier.

However, against the odds the Anglican Church underwent a revival of interest, in a movement centred on Oxford. It was soon labelled 'the Oxford Movement', headed by Oxford clergymen John Henry Newman, Edward Bouverie Pusey, John Keble and Henry Manning, among others. Their memorials in Oxford include Keble College and Pusey House, not to mention the Newman Society, aka the Oxford University Catholic Society, the oldest Catholic institution of the post-Reformation university.

To their enemies, the Oxford Movement's members were known as Tractarians, after a series of publications titled *Tracts for the Times*, published between 1833 and 1841. They were also called 'Newmanites' and 'Puseyites'. Like many former insulting terms, though – such as 'Methodism' a hundred years earlier – 'Tractarianism' became a respectable tag.

The Tractarians wanted the Anglican Church to return to its medieval roots, making the buildings colourful and inspiring like their Catholic counterparts, and also increasing the number of services and Communions. There was a renewed emphasis on the aesthetic and the meditational – things that had been stripped away by the dissenters at the other end of the Protestant scale. The 1836 church at Littlemore, built under the guidance of John Henry Newman, is a relic of these times.

The mood of Anglican revival spread to other parts of the county too, with vicar of Banbury William Wilson winning back large swathes of congregation from the Methodists and other nonconformists. In many poor villages, though, threats from the pulpit did not prevent parishioners attending dissenter services. The High Church ideals of Newman and his colleagues didn't penetrate much beyond Oxford.

It was all a spiritual push too far, and the Oxford Movement was accused of being Catholic in all but name. Accordingly, Newman made the final logical step and became a Catholic priest in 1845, followed by Henry Manning in 1851. That was the end of Tractarianism.

Newman was made a cardinal by the pope, and was one of the founders of the Catholic University of Ireland, which is now University College Dublin, the largest university in Ireland. He was beatified by Pope Benedict XVI on 19 September 2010, beatification being the last stage before full sanctification. It now requires one more miracle, involving the direct intercession of Newman's ghostly presence and confirmed by the Vatican, before he can be venerated as a Catholic saint.

DREAMING SPIRES AND OTHER BOARS

When poet Matthew Arnold visited Boar's Hill near Oxford in the 1840s with fellow poet Arthur Hugh Clough, the elevated spot offered uninterrupted fine views of the city. Arnold, who was later Oxford Professor of Poetry, hit upon a now timeless phrase in his poem *Thyrsis: A Monody*, 1865:

> ... And that sweet city with her dreaming spires,
> She needs not June for beauty's heightening,
> Lovely all times she lies, lovely to-night!

The poem was written in memory of Clough, and has sent several generations of romantics to the spot since publication; although ironically Clough himself had written of the site as barren and depressing beneath grey February skies. Boar's Hill was also the setting of Arnold's equally celebrated poem *The Scholar Gipsy*, a spot from which 'the eye travels down to Oxford's towers'.

Chilswell near Cumnor used to be called Childsworth, and Arnold uses that name in *Thyrsis*. The poem also mentions 'The signal-elm, that looks on Ilsley Downs'. The 'signal-elm' is still to be seen in a field near Chilswell (as is the best view of the dreaming spires), kept by the Oxford Preservation Society, which has a cluster of sites in the Boar's Hill vicinity. The tree is notable for the fact that it is not an elm at all, but an oak.

Poets have since made Boar's Hill their home, drawn here by Arnold's eulogy. Residents since the 1880s include Margaret Louisa Woods, Robert Bridges and John Masefield (successive Poet Laureates), along with Masefield's tenant Robert Graves, and Edmund Blunden, both destined to become Oxford Professors of Poetry.

FARMING CRISIS

The National Land Company (NLC), founded in 1845, bought 300 acres in Minster Lovell and called it Charterville, with the aim of attracting former farm labourers who had been lured away to the towns and cities. There were eighty smallholdings across 300 acres, complete with cottages and a share of forty oxen, eighteen pigs, manure, firewood and seed.

Charterville and the NLC were scuppered by more powerful landowners, who subjected it to the scrutiny of a Select Committee. The lottery system of allocating the land was outlawed, the company was wound up by Act of Parliament in 1851, and the plots had to be allocated via auction. In other words, the poor shareholders of the defunct NLC, the sole reason for the establishment of the allotments, couldn't afford to take part.

The original 'Charterville Allotments' survive as an area of neat bungalows with large gardens in the New Minster area of Minster Lovell.

In 1854, after two unusually wet years, the county's clay soils had become quagmires of dead crops, and livestock suffered with hoof rot. To recoup money lost in the failed harvest, many landowners cancelled tenancies and reduced the number of people working their land. More poor harvests in the 1850s and '60s combined with cheap imports to impoverish Oxfordshire farmers further. Tenants were suddenly hard to come by, and rents fell in an attempt to lure people back to the land. Several farms had to be amalgamated, and many acres of farmland were allowed to return to scrub, with former farm buildings left to decay.

In 1870 farm labourers formed an Oxfordshire branch of the National Union of Agricultural Workers (NUAW). No longer willing to take a passive role in the changes that had been thrust upon them, farmhands began to demand an increase in wages. One of their chief spokesmen was Christopher Holloway of Wootton. He pressed for a substantial hike in wages, from 11s to 16s. This was still a tiny amount – 16 shillings was equivalent to about £50 today, with 11s being a mere £35.

Rather than meet this demand, local farmers countered with the Oxford Association of Agriculturalists, refusing to increase the wage, and banning any union member from working their land. The farmhands went on strike, but the landowners simply brought in labourers from elsewhere. In Ascott-under-Wychwood sixteen women confronted a hired gang of blackleg workers from Ramsden, and were arrested, given a swift trial at Chipping Norton, and imprisoned in Oxford Castle with hard labour, on a charge of assault. Their children were looked after by neighbours, with NUAW assistance, during their incarceration.

The good folk of Chipping Norton rose up in protest, 1,000 of them gathering in an unsuccessful attempt to get the women released. Three thousand gathered in the town on the following day, where they were addressed by Joseph Arch, the most influential social reform speaker of the day. A whip-round coughed up £80 to support the women and their families.

Their efforts were eventually successful: questions in Parliament were followed by a royal pardon from Queen Victoria, who sent each woman 5s and a red flannel petticoat. The NUAW bettered this with £5 each and material to make a blue silk dress. The episode was used as a springboard to an investigation into labouring conditions on Oxfordshire farms.

The main consequence of stories like this was that even more people left the land. Four of the women upped sticks for New Zealand. In Wootton, forty families moved to industrial cities, most of them to Sheffield, and many more from Oxfordshire emigrated to America. In the 1880s the wage was finally raised – but only to 14s. When Victoria's reign came to an end, Oxfordshire farmhands were still only bringing home 14s and 11d a week – under £47 in today's money.

On a more positive note, Oxfordshire became a centre for agricultural innovations and improvement, following in the footsteps of Jethro Tull's seed drill a century earlier. Founded in 1811, the Oxfordshire Agricultural Society worked to improve the standard of stock-breeding. Robert Hobbs of Kelmscott led the way in sheep-rearing with his pedigree Shorthorns in the 1880s, and the new Oxford Downs breed was introduced across much of northern Oxfordshire. This sheep's inclusion on the Oxfordshire County Council coat of arms reflects its importance to the local economy. The arms were created in 1976 to reflect the reshaped county – an older version had included two of the animals.

Other local breeds developed at this time included the Oxford Sandy and Black pig, and the Oxford Brown hen. The former was in danger of disappearing in the twentieth century, but is now thriving again, largely due to the support of the Oxford Sandy and Black Society, formed in 1985 (after the Rare Breeds Survival Trust, formed in 1973, refused to recognise this pig as one worth saving).

Agricultural machinery was produced on a local scale in Oxfordshire. The Eagle Ironworks in Oxford was opened in 1760 by W. Lucy & Co., and in 1815 James Gardner of Banbury patented a turnip cutter which took off nationally. Gardner's business was sold to Sir Bernhard Samuelson in 1846, and was joined by a new line of reapers, mowers and sheaf binders, all produced at Banbury's Britannia Works (until its closure in 1933).

In 1868 Cowley entered its still-thriving era as a producer of machinery, with the foundation of John Allen and Co., makers of steam ploughs. These extraordinary machines worked in pairs, one at each side of the field, with a long plough slung between them. It was the death knell for the working horse, just as the working horse had been the death knell for farm oxen a hundred years earlier.

GRUBB LEADS TO BREAD RIOTS

Oxfordshire had encountered bread riots before. Poor harvests and avaricious millers conspired to inflate the price so much in 1693 that mobs took to the streets in Banbury, Chipping Norton, Charlbury, Oxford and elsewhere. Historian Anthony Wood noted in 1694 that 'divers starved to death in Oxford'.

The same problem recurred intermittently, but found its most violent expression in 1867. On 15 November that year the *Daily Telegraph* waxed purple, reporting:

Oxford in tumult and riotous confusion! Her stately streets
crowded with angry and starving people, her colleges shut up,
and two companies of Grenadier Guards, with forty pounds of
ammunition per man, bivouacked in her Corn Exchange! Such a
spectacle has scarcely been witnessed since the days when Rupert's
Cavaliers clattered through The High.

This tumult and riotous confusion all began with
Alderman Isaac Grubb, mayor of Oxford 1857–8. He
was the man who, in 1857, had put an end to the city's
annual humiliation on St Scholastica's Day (see page 84).
He owned several bread shops in Oxford, and was proud
of his contribution in providing the ordinary working
man with the basics of sustenance. But it was when he
began selling his bread to the university at prices lower
than those offered to the townsfolk – 7½d as opposed
to 9d for a large loaf – that his premises on Cornmarket
became the focus of bread riots.

It didn't take much to stir the mob-in-waiting's hatred
of the university into action, and it was ironic that it
should be champion of the people Isaac Grubb who bore
the brunt of their anger. In November 1867 *Jackson's
Oxford Journal* reported:

An immense crowd, numbering about 600 or 800 men and boys,
with a sprinkling of women, rushed along Cornmarket Street to
the shop of Alderman Grubb, baker, amidst hooting and yelling
and cries of 'We'll have our rights', 'We want cheap bread', etc. The
shop was, of course, closed; but the upper windows were speedily
riddled with stones and threats of firing his premises were made.

The bread rioters smashed windows in Grubb's
Cornmarket and Queen Street outlets, and in his

Summertown home too, before being scattered by the combined city and university authorities, with twenty or so being arrested. Various bits of the mob then turned on the colleges, putting rocks through windows.

A militia was called in – partly financed by none other than Isaac Grubb – comprising special constables and mounted Grenadier Guards from Windsor supplemented by special officers sourced locally. Magistrates issued an order for all boys to be kept indoors after 5 p.m. during the following week to avoid trouble. Students were told not to venture into Oxford after dark either. Pubs and shops were closed, and all musical bands and other means of drawing a crowd were banned. Even the scheduled performance in the Town Hall of *Jacob the Wizard* was cancelled. All grain stored in the town was removed by train for fear of theft.

On the 12th a crowd of thousands converged on Cornmarket to face the makeshift army, whose numbers totalled less than 200. Windows were broken, including at the police station. The angry mob mugged some students and smashed more windows during the next few days, outnumbering the hastily reinforced militia, and surging through the city streets a couple of thousand strong at the height of the protest. But alleged ringleaders were eventually brought to trial and variously fined, imprisoned or sent for hard labour. The town corporation eventually capitulated and told all Oxford bakers – Grubb included – to slice one penny off the price of a loaf.

MINOR MISDEMEANOURS AT THE OED

Oxford University drop-out Samuel Johnson may have given the English language its first dictionary, but it was

James Augustus Henry Murray (1837–1915) who gave it the one that would stand for ever as a monument to the language. He began work on the first *Oxford English Dictionary* (OED) in 1878, with an approach that is very familiar to us in this Wikipedia age, but quite revolutionary at the time – the soliciting of contributions.

One man alone would not have enough hours in his lifetime to complete a work of this magnitude; but a few hundred likeminded lexicographers could see the job through – especially in a city that had the vast resources of the Bodleian Library in its midst.

Moving to Oxford in 1884, Murray built a 'Scriptorium' in his back yard on Banbury Road. Slips of paper with literary and other quotations arrived by the sack load, and even letters addressed with a minimalist 'Mr Murray, Oxford' found their way to him. The post generated by this backyard industry was such that the Post Office installed a bespoke postbox (still standing) outside the house.

Amongst Murray's army of enthusiastic amateur researchers was the prolific Dr W.C. Minor, who eventually contributed 12,000 quotations for the project. Organising a celebratory Dictionary Dinner at Oxford in October 1897, Murray was keen to meet and invite the elusive doctor.

Disappointingly, the story goes, Minor replied saying he was too ill to attend, but invited Murray to come to a mansion in Crowthorne, Berkshire. Murray took up the invitation, and was ushered into an impressively book-stuffed study. Approaching the respectable looking middle-aged gentleman who occupied the room, Murray declared what a pleasure it was to meet at last his indispensable contributor.

The owner of the mansion shook his hand, but announced that his name was Nicholson, and that he was the governor of Broadmoor Asylum for the Clinically Insane, just down the road in Crowthorne. Dr Minor, an American and former army surgeon, was his longest-serving inmate, committed after being found guilty of murder.

Murray did eventually meet W.C. Minor – several times, in fact – but the meeting at the governor's house is, sadly, a piece of well-structured fiction.

In reality, Murray appears to have become aware of his star contributor's unusual circumstances in 1889 when an American scholar made a chance remark about 'Poor Dr Minor'. The facts tumbled forth and came as a great surprise to Murray, even though he had been sending correspondence to Minor for ten years using the address 'Broadmoor, Crowthorne, Berkshire'. He always assumed, given the 'Doctor' tag, that his man was a medical officer at the prison. Shocked, but keeping an admirably stiff upper lip, Murray noted of this revelation:

> I was of course deeply affected by the story, but as Dr. Minor had never in the least alluded to himself or his position, all I could do was to write to him more respectfully and kindly than before, so as to show no notice of this disclosure, which I feared might make some change in our relations.

The men met for the first time in 1891, and Murray visited, and wrote, constantly from then until his death, their conversations always centring on the dictionary.

It was his large stash of sixteenth- and seventeenth-century volumes that provided the meat for Minor's major research. He sometimes delivered over 100 entries a week. Murray once declared of Minor's contributions 'that we could easily illustrate the last four centuries from his quotations alone'.

This unique bedrock of the OED died in 1920, while Murray passed away five years earlier at his Oxford home.

WILLIAM MORRIS: ELUSIVE UTOPIA

The artist William Morris, educated at Exeter College in Oxford, is remembered largely for his curtain and wall-paper patterns, like some nineteenth-century forerunner of Laura Ashley. But Morris's designs were revolutionary in their day, and that is a more accurate image of the man. He founded the Socialist League in 1884, and advocated a new society based on a shared love of nature; an absence of money, property and class; and all the other trappings of socialist utopia.

These ideas were expressed in his novel *News from Nowhere* (1890), whose setting was inspired by the sixteenth-century Kelmscott House, Morris's spiritual home, which he bought and furnished in 1871, and where he was buried in 1896. He named his London residence Kelmscott House in honour of the village, and founded the Kelmscott Press there as a showcase of his artistry.

Oxford's Jane Burdon was born on 19 October 1839 in St Helen's Passage (leading from New College Lane to the Turf Tavern). Its alternative name was Hell Passage, a comment on its slums. But Burdon's was a Cinderella tale, and at the age of 18 her striking features won her the hearts of Pre-Raphaelite Brotherhood painters Dante

Gabriel Rossetti and Edward Burne-Jones. She was roped in to pose as Guinevere in their Oxford Union Arthurian murals.

Another member of the Brotherhood was William Morris. Rossetti fell in love with Burdon, but it was Morris who married her, at St Michael's church, Cornmarket, in 1859. After this, glass slipper firmly in place, Burdon was educated and socially equipped for her new status; and she became the one and only female face for the Pre-Raphaelite artists, appearing in dozens of paintings.

Things began to unwind in 1871 when Morris and Rossetti rented Kelmscott Manor in Oxfordshire, and Rossetti and Burdon fell into a love affair. She survived the turmoil; and, rich and famous, she outlived the men and eventually bought the manor in 1913 for her daughter. She is buried in the village churchyard; and there is a blue plaque to her in St Helen's Passage.

STONEY BROKE AT HEADINGTON

The once-thriving quarries at Headington, and elsewhere in Oxfordshire, were reduced to supplying rubble for roads by the mid-nineteenth century. Gone were the days when every new decade brought a new university building which demanded the finest stone – a demand that had been the foundation of the Oxford suburb of Headington Quarry.

Headington had a backup plan, however, with its brickworks taking up the slack as the quarries declined. It was a hand-to-mouth existence for the men who worked there, and this in part explains the strength and popularity of the Morris dancing tradition in Headington Quarry. The link might not seem obvious, until you realise that Morris sides were not established to dance some romantic dream of Ye Olde England, but simply to raise extra money for poor families, and to make inroads into their extensive beer tabs.

Headington Quarry looms large in the story of Morris dancing and the English folk song revival due to a chance encounter that took place on Boxing Day in 1899. Folk song collector Cecil Sharpe heard the Quarry Morris team playing under his window while he was staying as a guest at Sandfield Cottage in Headington (on a site currently covered by Horwood Close). The Morris-men-cum-brickmakers, led by William Kimber on concertina, did not usually play at this time of year, but a bad season at the brickworks had forced them to go busking.

Sharpe was fascinated by the music he heard, and asked Kimber to call on him the following day so that he could note down the tunes. This in turn inspired him to search for more musical treasures, kick-starting an English folk song revival that continued into the 1950s, with collectors noting hundreds of songs and tunes that might otherwise have died out unrecorded.

There is a faded plaque on Horwood Close commemorating this quietly revolutionary meeting, and a blue plaque commemorating Kimber was unveiled in 2011 on the house he built with his own bricks on St Anne's Road, Headington. His grave, with a concertina motif, is in Headington Quarry churchyard, close to that of C.S. Lewis.

There were additional brick-making sites at Wheatley, Nettlebed and Woodstock. But the other important stone material in the region was Stonesfield slate. This had been an important roofing material since the thirteenth century, and by the nineteenth century its preparation had taken on an almost ritualistic nature. The stone was quarried, and then laid out on the ground and covered in turf. Keen eyes kept a watch on the weather, and as soon as a hard frost was forecast, the Stonesfield church bells were rung, and the turf was removed by all the men of the village, and the stone laid out ready to receive the elements. The ensuing frost would split the stone along its natural bedding planes, and it was then ready for shaping into roof slate.

THE MORRIS MAYOR

In 1885 Thomas Hemming of Abingdon, the Mayor of Ock Street, resigned after twenty-five years in power. The title passed to his son, William, who inherited a rare survival of a once widespread tradition – the office of Mock Mayor. This dubious individual's job was to voice the will of the common people, in the days before they had any means of formal representation, and to satirise the official mayor.

The Mayor of Ock Street still exists in the twenty-first century, but candidates should be warned that the mayor's power is limited: the only intervention he is allowed to make in the everyday running of local life is 'to turn an old sow out of the gutter and take her place himself', according to the rule book.

The Mayor of Ock Street title is the preserve of the Abingdon Traditional Morris. Their version of the story says that in 1700 an Abingdonian named Morris organised an ox-roast and distributed the food to the poor.

The benison was so good that fights broke out to claim the ox's horns. Opposing sides formed on either side of the Ock Street–Vineyard divide. On 21 June 1700 the Ock Street faction claimed victory.

Since then, the Morris men have carried these horns in their midst, mounted on a wooden, garlanded ox-head effigy. The fight is commemorated each year on the Saturday nearest 19 June with dancing, a small fair, and the election of the Mayor of Ock Street, official keeper of the horns. All residents of Ock Street (site of the Morland Brewery from 1711 to 1999) can vote, and the mayor acts as Squire of Abingdon Traditional Morris for a year. His sword of office is said to have been carved from a cudgel used in the original brawl.

Abingdon's eccentricities do not end there. Whenever there is an occasion of local or national celebration, buns are launched from the roof of the town's County Hall Museum. No one is quite sure why, but there have been at least thirty-five such edible bombardments since 1761, when bread was made airborne to mark the coronation of George III. Events warranting rolls on the drum over the last few years have been the Queen's 90th birthday in 2016, and the 100th anniversary of the end of the First World War in November 2018. The origins and significance of this tradition have been lost, but a collection of varnished buns, some of them 200 years old, can be seen in the museum.

10

THE TWENTIETH CENTURY

In the early twentieth century Oxfordshire underwent the industrial and population growth typical of much of the country – although the population grew much slower here than elsewhere in England. The urban migration was partly fuelled by Oxfordshire having lower wages than any other county. Being so rural, the region had largely missed out on the full impact of the Industrial Revolution that had upped wages elsewhere. Its cottage industries of lace- and glove-making could not compete with factory-scale rivals elsewhere.

Bigger employers included the blanket and tweed factories in Witney, cement works at Chinnor and Shipton-on-Cherwell, iron ore extraction in quarries at Bloxham, Hook Norton and Wroxton, and the Northern Aluminium factory at Banbury. There were also big breweries in the county, notably Morland in Abingdon, Morrells and Halls in Oxford, Hunt Edmunds in Banbury, and Hook Norton. Only the latter has survived. There were several RAF bases in the county too.

The biggest of the new urban employers was Morris Motors Limited and the associated Pressed Steel Company in Cowley, both spearheaded by William Morris (later

Lord Nuffield). Between them these companies employed thousands. In its modern guise as BMW's Mini plant (known as Plant Oxford, and complemented by Plant Swindon a few miles to the west), the car business is still an important part of the city's economy. Oxford Business Park occupies a large section of the former Morris plant.

In spite of quarrying, Wroxton retains its timeless charm.

Morris made another skyline-altering impact on Oxford, with Nuffield College, originally mooted in 1937. The New Road canal basin and coal wharves had been filled in to provide the site; but the plans had to be scaled down due to problems with budget and lack of materials in post-war Britain. The 'temporary' car park over the road from the college is a lingering result of this shortfall – it only exists because the college was unable to extend its sprawl westwards over Worcester Street.

Morris' plans were approved in 1940, and work finally began in 1949; but the college was not completed until 1960. Initially funded solely by Morris, in the late 1950s the Nuffield Foundation charity was set up to provide more money.

Women, who had been allowed to study in Oxford for forty-five years, were finally allowed to take Oxford University degrees in 1920; and the rise of the institution currently known as Oxford Brookes University brought an even greater influx of students to the city.

The M40 motorway was constructed between 1967 and 1974, with the section between Oxford and Birmingham opening in 1990. Its birth had not been easy. Protesters mauled the original plans, which involved the wholesale destruction of one of Oxfordshire's jewels of recreated wilderness, Otmoor. Part of the ultimately successful campaign against the original route involved selling more than 3,000 small sections of a field to worldwide buyers to raise funds. The piecemeal field had been evocatively named Alice's Field, in reference to local author Lewis Carroll and his famous literary creation.

William Carter bought land from the Duke of Marlborough in 1900, selling parcels of it to people who wanted to build their own houses. This was the origin of Carterton, named after William Carter. It got off to a poor start, with neighbouring Black Bourton perversely hindering attempts to have running water and electricity supplied to the new settlement. Prior to the Second World War its main contribution to the economy was locally grown tomatoes. Some of these Carterton fruits sank in the kitchens of the *Titanic* in 1912.

Blenheim Palace's most famous son Winston Churchill died on 30 January 1965. His demise was greeted by national mourning ('I am ready to meet my maker. Whether my maker is prepared for the ordeal of meeting me is another matter,' he had previously commented). His body was taken to Hanborough railway station by a locomotive called, appropriately enough, *Winston Churchill*, and the funeral procession continued by road to Bladon. The shadow cast by Churchill over the twentieth century had been longer than any other, and it was very much the end of an era.

EDWARDIAN EMPIRE BUILDING

Edward VII started his academic career at Christ Church College, Oxford in 1859, transferring to Trinity College, Cambridge in 1861. Oxford commemorated its association with the king by opening a new pub, the Edward VII, on Vicarage Road. It closed in 1991. The eagle-eyed will also spot one or two of the twelve surviving Oxford postboxes from this era too – often overlooked as they have 'ER' on them, leading to the assumption that they are the initials of Queen Elizabeth. The Roman numeral 'VII' is the giveaway.

Related to most other European royal families through his siblings, Edward was fondly known as the 'uncle of Europe'. He also presided over an age in which Britain ruled the largest empire in the world, whose prime movers were educated at Oxford. It was a time of brief, over-inflated grandeur before the descent into the hell of the First World War.

Frank Lascelles of Sibford Gower was known as 'The Man Who Staged the Empire'. His real name was Frank Stevens, son of the local vicar. He adopted the new surname to reflect his exotic calling – pageantry. Lascelles was, indeed, the pioneer of pageants, a short-lived fad involving cast-heavy spectaculars which gained popularity in the Edwardian era. His shows brought the glories of the British Empire to any theatre or marquee that would accommodate him.

Lascelles choreographed huge numbers of people in his extravaganzas. His first production, in 1907, was called the 'Oxford Historical', and it went down well with the general public in spite of opposition from Oxford University, who objected to the huge crowds involved both on and off stage. There was even an old-fashioned student riot, like in the good old days of Town versus Gown.

Lascelles' scale grew ever bigger – 15,000 at the Pageant of London, and 300,000 at the Coronation Durbar pageant in Calcutta. Whenever an empire theme was mooted for a celebration, Lascelles was wheeled out as Master of the Pageant. He died in 1934, at his self-designed mansion, the Manor House, in Sibford Gower.

THE FIRST WORLD WAR:
IT ALL STARTED IN SUTTON COURTENAY

Sutton Courtenay near Abingdon has the very dubious honour of being the place where Britain's part in the First World War formally began. Prime Minister Herbert Asquith, educated at Balliol College in Oxford and later given the title Lord Oxford, had bought Walton House on the edge of the village in 1912, building his main residence The Wharf next door. Here he signed the declaration that plunged the country into conflict. Asquith remained in the village after his resignation in 1916, and is buried there in All Saints' churchyard.

Morris Motors and the Pressed Steel Company in Cowley employed thousands of people from Oxford and beyond, the car factory producing 650 tanks in the First World War, while the Pressed Steel Company, normally turning out steel car bodies, churned out thousands of cartridge cases, employing a largely female workforce.

Two of the ancient trades of Oxfordshire, weaving and glove-making, had a new lease of life in the war. Woodstock, Witney, Burford and Chipping Norton had weathered the economic and social upheavals and were still producing goods from wool and animal skins. As a snapshot of their importance at this time, in the build-up to hostilities in 1914 a single order for 70,000 leather army-grade gloves was made in Woodstock, bringing the glovers 4 or 5 pence a pair, which is approximately £1 or £1.25 in today's money.

A former toll bridge now known as the Airmen's Bridge crosses the Thames at Wolvercote. It has a plaque commemorating an accident which took place there in 1912 when the adjoining Port Meadow was a military airfield. Two officers of the Royal Flying Corps were killed in a plane crash, and 2,226 Oxfordians gave money to fund the plaque.

During the two world wars the university colleges became temporary military barracks, training grounds and hospitals – just as they had been 300 years earlier during the Civil Wars. Oxford avoided damage in both conflicts, though, lacking the heavy industry or strategic targets that first the Zeppelins and then the Luftwaffe were seeking.

The thirteenth-century Lakenhalle or Cloth Hall at Ypres in Belgium, the largest commercial building of the Middle Ages, was flattened during artillery fire in the First World War. After the conflict, one of the Roman 'I' numerals from the hall's shattered tower clock made its way to Westwell near Burford, where Lady Stetta Aimee Holland, wife of the lord of the manor at Westwell, incorporated it into the war memorial beside the picturesque village pond. It was specifically in memory of her brothers Harold and John Price, who had been killed during the war, even though they had no connection with Westwell, other than their sister.

Members of the Oxfordshire and Buckinghamshire Light Infantry had taken part in the bitter First Battle of

Ypres in 1914, along with the equally devastating Battle of Passchendaele near Ypres in 1917. The Westwell memorial is an apt reminder of this connection.

Although its history stretches back to before the Norman Conquest, Caversfield's population had seldom reached three figures until 1911 when Bicester Airfield, later RAF Bicester, installed servicemen on Skimmington Lane. The RAF moved out in 2004 and the old houses are now used by the MOD's Defence Logistics Organisation, which has since become part of an amalgamated organisation, Defence Equipment and Support. Airmen from the US Air Force, based at RAF Croughton in Northamptonshire, live in the parish too.

Oddington church on the edge of Otmoor has an unusual feature at its west side: a statue of Mary and Jesus (a pieta) decorated with brightly gurning Māori totems. This is a memorial to the Māori servicemen who took part in the First World War. It was installed by Margaret Papakura (aka Makereti), a resident of mixed Māori-British parentage who settled in the village. She took part in the war effort by assisting recuperating soldiers from New Zealand, and was buried in Oddington church. The grave is a place of pilgrimage for New Zealanders keen to acknowledge her contribution to Māori culture; and items from her Kiwi cultural collection are kept at the Pitt Rivers Museum in Oxford.

SHELL SHOCK HORROR

The casualties of war were in full view in Oxford. The Thames carried boatloads of convalescent soldiers; the Examination Schools were full of hospital wards, overflowing with wounded men; and in the grounds of New College there was a shanty town of hospital tents, housing soldiers suffering from shell shock.

Psychological disorder was the specialist area of Oxford academic William McDougall, who held the university post of Wilde Reader in Mental Philosophy between 1904 and 1920. He had observed the new phenomenon of 'shell shock' – for which several men had already been unfairly executed on the front line – the severe mental illness crudely interpreted as cowardice and desertion.

One anonymous patient whose story helped McDougall shape his diagnosis had been on the front line for two years, surviving both the battles of Mons and the Somme. He was said to have gone 'over the top' in battle nineteen times, had been caught in a British friendly fire artillery barrage, and had seen most of his comrades die. On his final mission he had fought his way to a shelled German dugout and taken prisoners. A British officer then arrived, and shot all the prisoners with his revolver. This sent the soldier over the edge, with the first symptoms of shell shock – uncontrollable trembling, involuntary twitching, weeping, and an overwhelming sense of panic.

Shell shock had first been described two years previously, as 'an orgy of neuroses and psychoses and gaits and paralyses', and was thought to be the result of an invasion of the central nervous system or the brain – either from toxic gases or tiny fragments of explosives. McDougall was one of the first to realise that the syndrome was a psychological disorder brought on by exposure to trench warfare and the horrors it inflicted on the human senses.

McDougall's patient had been making good progress, but one night a section of the ancient town wall in the New College grounds collapsed noisily, and his symptoms had returned in force.

The eminent psychologist's interest in his subjects was purely academic, though. Renowned as arrogant and aloof, McDougall advocated 'positive eugenics' of the sort espoused by many proto-fascists in the pre-Holocaust era, horrified at the huge families raised by the average working-class couple. The aim was to filter out low intellect, and McDougall proposed improving the bright spark/two short planks ratio by offering university dons, civil servants and other members of the intelligentsia financial incentives for raising big families. Leading from the front but stalling, he only managed to produce five children himself.

WAR GOES FROM BAD TO VERSE

Oxford enjoyed more peacetime in the First World War than the rest of Britain. Due to inefficient communications, news of the declaration of war took more than two days to reach Oxford Town Hall.

The lack of Zeppelin attacks on Oxford was attributed by writer Joseph Wells in 1920 to silence – particularly the silence of Christ Church's bell, Great Tom:

> During the war Tom was forbidden to sound, along with all the other Oxford bells and clocks, for might not his mighty voice have guided some Zeppelin or German aeroplane to pour down destruction on Oxford? Few things brought home more to Oxford the meaning of the Armistice than hearing Tom once more on the night of November 11, 1918.

Prime Minister-to-be Harold Macmillan was wounded three times in the war, and never returned to complete his degree at Balliol. He commented later, 'I could not face it. It was a city of ghosts.'

He was one of the lucky survivors. Some 2,700 Oxford University men were killed in the 1914–18 conflict – 18 per cent of 15,000 or so members who had enlisted. Corpus Christi College lost 25 per cent of its members, while New College lost the most individuals – 257.

The Wilfred Owen Archive is kept by Oxford University. Owen was one of the less fortunate combatants, killed just a week before the Armistice. He had made the decision to remain at the front to chronicle the war, taking the place of fellow poet, friend and mentor Siegfried Sassoon (a one-time Oxford resident) who had been wounded in the head during an unfortunate incident of 'friendly fire'. Sassoon was horrified, threatening to stab Owen in order to invalid him out of the army.

Other war poets with Oxford connections include Lincoln College alumnus Edward Thomas, whose eulogy to the city, *Oxford*, was published in 1903. Like Owen, he died during the conflict.

NOTES FROM THE SECOND WORLD WAR

Hitler's decision not to bomb Oxford was said to be based on the city's central location and his admiration of its beautiful architecture. He had earmarked it as his main base in England following German victory in the war.

Edward F. Halifax, viceroy to India and ambassador to America, stated soon after the Second World War:

'I often think how much easier the world would have been to manage if Herr Hitler and Signor Mussolini had been at Oxford.'

Writer Vera Brittain (1893–1970), alumnus of Somerville College, lost most of her loved ones in the First World War, including her fiancé and brother. She became a nursing auxiliary, studied in Oxford again after the war, and became a successful writer and public speaker. Her fame as a 'principled pacifist' and her influential voice on the international stage is underlined beautifully by her inclusion in Hitler's notorious Black Book, which named 2,000 people to be immediately arrested in Britain after the Germans invaded.

Penicillin was developed in Oxford during the war as the world's first antibiotic. First described by Alexander Fleming in 1925, it was Nazi Germany refugee Ernst Chain and Rhodes Scholar Howard Florey who developed it as a drug fit for mass production. Their guinea pig was an Oxford policeman who was dying from an infected wound inflicted while pruning roses. The drug worked near-miracles, but supplies ran out. Traces were recycled from the policeman's urine, but not enough to save his life.

Demolished in 2004, the papermill at Lower Wolvercote used to supply the Oxford University Press, and provide the material upon which *Jackson's Oxford Journal* (1782–1928) was printed. Powered solely by the Thames until 1811, it then utilised a steam engine requiring 100 tons of coal a week. The main purpose of the Oxford Canal was to transport coal for such purposes as this. Members of the university and Oxford University Press were employed to write and produce pro-Allies propaganda leaflets in German – all printed on Wolvercote paper, of course.

The Oxford University Air Squadron (OUAS) was the source of many fighters in the Battle of Britain, including Spitfire ace Richard Hillary, shot down twice in 1939 after taking down several enemy planes. Rising again from extensive plastic surgery – an area pioneered at Oxford – he was shot down for the last time in 1943.

The most famous member of the OUAS was Group Captain Leonard Cheshire. Awarded the Victoria Cross, it was after his 103rd mission as official British observer of the nuclear bombing of Nagasaki that his life changed. From then on he poured his money and efforts into charitable works, the most lasting being the health and welfare charity the Leonard Cheshire Foundation (called Leonard Cheshire Disability since 2007).

During the Second World War, Begbroke had a unique unit of Air Raid Precautions (ARP) wardens, made up of Servite friars. They were based at the eighteenth-century Begbroke Manor House, which had become part of the Roman Catholic Priory of St Philip in the 1880s. (It remained a base for novice Servite friars until 2000. There were also Servite would-be nuns in Begbroke until 1984, when St Juliana's Convent School closed due to structural issues and cashflow problems.)

The clock on the 1794 church tower at Benson is marked out in Roman numerals, and has XI at both the 11 and the 9 positions. This error was used to fiendish effect by Irish-raised American British Union of Fascists member William Joyce, aka Lord Haw-Haw, in the Second World War. Working for Nazi Germany's English-language propaganda programme *Germany Calling*, Joyce announced to a cowed Britain that there would be an air raid on 'an airfield near the village whose clock had two elevens'. Riddle-busters failed to crack the code, and RAF Benson was bombed.

During the Second World War, Hatford's off-licence received a direct hit from a German bomb. A girl was killed in the blast, along with two boys from London. In the darkest of ironies, they had been evacuated there to escape the London Blitz.

The RAF base at Barford St John only lasted four years, between 1942 and 1946, but the site has since been taken over by the United States Air Force, which has a communications centre on the old airfield, linked to the enormously numbered 2130th Communications Squadron at RAF Croughton in Northamptonshire. From this base the USAF deals with an estimated one third of all the USA's military communications in Europe.

Wallingford was saved from disaster in 1944 by self-sacrificing airmen. When a Royal Canadian Air Force Halifax bomber caught fire whilst flying over the town, most of the crew bailed out. But Flying Officer Wilding and Sergeant Andrew stayed on board. The aircraft was carrying its full capacity of bombs, and would have left a large hole in the town. The two men steered the flaming plane to a nose-dive in an isolated field near Crowmarsh. An obelisk at the junction of Wilding Road and Andrew Road in Wallingford commemorates the event.

During the Second World War a 3.5-mile railway was built by German prisoners of war to link a series of iron-stone quarries with the mainline. This was the heyday of the Oxfordshire Ironstone Company, which operated between 1917 and 1978, quarrying one of the biggest ore fields in the country. At its height it was churning out 40,000 tons of ore per week. But the boom came and went, and today the only functional expression of the old industry is the Ironstone Benefice. This is a group of churches lying along the old quarrying grounds, at Alkerton, Balscote, Drayton, Hanwell, Horley, Shenington and Wroxton.

FLASHES OF SILLINESS

'Mistrust a man who never has an occasional flash of silliness,' said the Right Honourable Sir Gerald Hugh Tyrwhitt-Wilson, aka the 14th Lord Berners (1883–1950), composer, novelist and painter, and owner of Faringdon House. He clearly had the Tyrwhitt to woo and followed his own dictum. He was responsible for the still-extant tradition of pigeon-dyeing. He was also fond of erecting signs along the lines of 'Do not throw stones at this notice' and 'Mangling done here'.

Berners' output includes the immortal verse:

> Red Roses blow but thrice a year,
> In June, July or May:
> But owners of Red Noses
> Can blow them every day.

During the Second World War the 43m-high tower on Faringdon (or Folly) Hill was used by the Home Guard as a lookout post, affording views across the surrounding Vale of the White Horse. It was built as a folly in 1935 by Lord Berners, little suspecting the practical use it would be put to a few years later. In 1982 Robert Heber-Percy restored the tower and donated it to the town of Faringdon.

LITERARY LARKS

Juniper Hill near Cottisford, just south of the Northamptonshire border, was the birthplace of Flora Thompson (1876–1947). She renamed the hamlet Lark Rise in her semi-autobiographical books, Cottisford itself becoming Fordlow. Her other key locations were Buckingham (Candleford) and Fringford (Candleford Green). The books capture lives at once ordinary and meaningful, soaked in a rich four-season marinade of quintessential Englishness, a marriage of Vaughan Williams and Camberwick Green.

The *Lark Rise* trilogy (*Heatherley*, a sequel, appeared posthumously) started life as a series of essays published by Oxford University Press in 1938–43 as a healing balm to a nation suffering in wartime. Since then it has never been out of print, and it has inspired stage shows, music and the popular *Lark Rise* television series screened between 2008 and 2011 (and filmed in Gloucestershire and Wiltshire rather than Oxfordshire).

By all accounts, Poet Laureate John Betjeman (1906–84) did not enjoy his studies at Magdalen College in Oxford. But his stint there left its mark on literature. Amongst his college baggage was a teddy bear called Archibald Ormsby-Gore, who caught the eye of fellow student Evelyn Waugh. Waugh later cast Ormsby-Gore as Aloysius, the teddy bear of Sebastian Flyte in *Brideshead Revisited*.

Betjeman himself captured the Oxford era in his long narrative poem *Summoned by Bells*, and his other work includes many references to Oxfordshire. But he never quite recovered from his academic failures in the city, levelling particular ire at tutor C.S. Lewis. The only qualification he ever wrested from the university was an honorary doctorate, handed over in 1974.

Betjeman set his children's book *Archie and the Strict Baptists* in Uffington and Farnborough (in Warwickshire), the scenes of his childhood. The Archie in question is that self-same bear Ormsby-Gore who, along with another favourite toy, Jumbo the elephant, was in Betjeman's arms when he died.

From 1972 until his death in 1984 Betjeman lived in Wantage. Wantage repaid its debt with the Betjeman Millennium Park, where his poem 'On Leaving Wantage' is carved in stone.

Oxford professor and Narnia creator Clive Staples Lewis was known as Jack to his friends and family. At the age of 4 he had lost his pet dog Jacksie in a road accident, and insisted on adopting the animal's name as his own. The love of animals stayed with him, and he claimed that his earliest literary and creative influences were the anthropomorphic creations of Beatrix Potter.

The writer's biggest legacy in modern Oxford is the C.S. Lewis Nature Reserve at Risinghurst in Oxford, formerly part of the grounds of his house The Kilns, a private residence with a blue plaque to the famous scholar-author. But on the international stage he is known primarily for his Narnia books, and his many writings on Christianity, having converted from atheism, largely under the influence of his devout friend J.R.R. Tolkien.

Tolkien was a pipe-smoking Oxford University academic who had no interest in fame and celebrity, and yet who, in 2009, was judged the highest-earning dead writer in the world, on account of book sales and other Middle Earth merchandise and movie-related goods.

The Kilns, former home of C.S. Lewis.

In life Tolkien was Rawlinson and Bosworth Professor of Anglo-Saxon at Oxford University from 1925 to 1945, and Merton Professor of English Language and Literature from then until 1959, with earlier stints writing for the *Oxford English Dictionary*. A student of Exeter College, as a professor he was based first at Pembroke, and then at Merton. Oxford currently has a J.R.R. Tolkien Professor of English Literature and Language post in memory of the man's work and influence.

Tolkien is buried with his wife Edith in the cemetery at Wolvercote in north Oxford, and there are blue plaques on his one-time residences at 76 Sandfield Road and 20 Northmoor Road in suburban Oxford. His favourite city watering hole, The Eagle and Child, on St Giles, is a busy beery shrine for pilgrims of Tolkien and C.S. Lewis.

Beyond Oxford, one of Tolkien's favourite pubs was The Bell inn at Charlbury. Drinking here in the 1950s, with his name in the literary firmament following the success of *The Lord of the Rings*, he overheard the landlord bemoaning his treatment by the brewery and wishing he could buy out the lease. Feeling magnanimous, Tolkien declared, 'I might be able to help you there, you know.' Not knowing who he was, the landlord assessed his customer's shabby jacket, wafted away the clouds of pipe smoke and replied sadly, 'Oh no, I don't think you can', blowing what was probably his only chance of breaking free from the brewery yoke.

Sutton Courtenay's All Saints' church is the last resting place of author George Orwell (1903–50). As a boy he had frequented the area, sometimes fishing in the river; but the village was not the obvious choice of final resting place. Henley-on-Thames or Shiplake, where he spent some of his early years, might have been more appropriate.

Orwell's posthumous journey to Sutton was convoluted. Legend says that he wanted to be buried in the churchyard nearest to whichever place he died. Passing away in London, it seemed that the choice would be endless. The funeral service took place at Christ Church near Regent's Park; but the city could not find space for him, and cremation seemed the only option – a fate that Orwell had expressly forbidden.

David Astor, Orwell's old friend from the *Observer* newspaper, stepped in. Based in palatial accommodation at Sutton Courtenay, Astor commanded the ear of the village vicar. Orwell was duly interred, with his real name Eric Arthur Blair inscribed on the headstone as he had instructed. Astor was later buried there too, alongside his old friend.

KINGS OF THE ROAD

William Morris, owner of Morris Motors and creator of 'affordable motoring', was born in 1877, in a terraced house in Cowley near Oxford. These everyman beginnings never entirely left him, and he continued to be a philanthropic benefactor and instigator, even when untold wealth had removed him several strata, socially, from his modest beginnings. And even though he was, by all accounts, neither warm nor charismatic, just endlessly practical.

His business breakthrough came at the age of 16 with a bicycle repair business in the shed at the bottom of the family garden. Having shifted from bikes to cars, he designed his first commercial model, the Morris Oxford (aka the Bullnose Morris), in 1912, moving the workshop to a disused military training college in Cowley soon after. The 'affordable motoring' concept literally changed the nature of Britain's roads, bringing motor vehicles within reach of a broad cross-section of the population.

During the First World War the Cowley works produced munitions, just as it was to manufacture Spitfires and Tiger Moths in the Second bout, and Morris' star was firmly in the firmament. He was knighted in 1929, and became Lord Nuffield in 1934. In the preceding year he had moved to Nuffield Place near Henley-on-Thames, inspiring the choice of title.

By 1937 Morris Motors Ltd was the largest motor manufacturer in Europe. The inflow of money into the Nuffield coffers was unstoppable. Morris founded Nuffield College in this year, even though it was not completed until 1960 due to building 'rationing' during the post-war rearmament drive. In 1943 the Nuffield Foundation was set up with a kick-start of £10 million. Indeed, it is said that William Morris gave away the equivalent in today's money of £11 billion. He died in 1963.

The BMW Mini is currently made on the site of the Morris works. The motor industry has other Oxfordshire links too. MG cars used to be produced in Abingdon: the factory closed in 1980 after fifty-one years.

Wykeham Mill in Bloxham was once a king of the road too, producing vehicles such as the Jaguar XJ220 supercar and the Aston Martin DB7. The mill is now occupied by Vantage Business Park, named after the last Aston Martin produced there, the DB7 V12 Vantage. The headline in the *Banbury Guardian* for 5 December 2003, which foreshadowed the car plant's closure, announced 'End of the line for 007's super car'.

Formula One is still parked locally. Virgin F1 has its technical base in Bicester; and Lotus Renault F1 has its chassis designed and built at Enstone, with the car engines coming from Viry-Châtillon near Paris.

F1 teams liaise closely with Oxford Brookes School of Technology which, along with Oxford and Cranfield universities, is part of Faraday Advance. This takes an innovative, scientific look at future technology, looking for an equal ratio of low pollution to high efficiency in all forms of transport.

But the real 'super car' is the one being fitted out by Oxford YASA Motors. The company has developed engines for high-performance electronic vehicles, and YASA is also leading the way in the post-fossil fuel aerospace and industrial sectors. The pro-petrol lobby, still chuckling at memories of wobbly Sinclair C5s, needs to digest the implications of the YASA 750 electric motor: it accelerates from 0 to 60mph in three seconds and enables a top speed of 140mph.

OXFAM: THE FIRST FOOD BANK

The embryonic Oxford Committee for Famine Relief held its first meeting public in the library of the Church of St Mary the Virgin in Oxford in 1942. The organisers, all likeminded Quakers, were concerned that the British government's policy of preventing the importation of food supplies into German-controlled mainland Europe was causing hardship to the oppressed civilians. The Oxford Committee, along with others throughout Britain, urged the government to allow controlled distribution to civilians under the guiding hand of the International Red Cross, their specific concern being the people of occupied Greece, known to be dying in their thousands through starvation.

After the war, as Oxfam, the committee continued to organise collections of food and clothing when all the other wartime organisations had folded, and by the late 1950s it was active in most of the poorer parts of the world. The headquarters of Oxfam GB are still in Oxford, at Cowley, and it employs more than 6,000 people world-wide. There is a blue plaque commemorating founder and first Honorary Secretary Cecil Jackson-Cole (1901–79) at 17 Broad Street.

COLD WAR FOOLS AND SPIES

A tiny museum of bygones relating to the splendidly titled villages of Filkins and Broughton Poggs is kept in a seventeenth-century cottage in Filkins. It is called the Swinford Museum, after its founder George, who established it in the 1930s with the help of Labour MP Sir Stafford Cripps (who lived locally).

Cripps was one of the politicians who welcomed a Soviet delegation of jet engine designers in 1946, seeking help with their faltering projects back home in the USSR. Sir Stafford, with a benevolent nod from his party, allowed them to study Rolls-Royce jet engine technology, and discussed a licence by which they could produce versions of the engine for Soviet planes. This resulted in the Klimov vk-1 jet engine, used in the MiG-15s that fought against UN forces in North Korea in the 1950s, much to the dismay of the b-29 bombers they targeted.

All of which had come as a great shock to Josef Stalin. When his jet engineers first approach him with the proposal to contact the UK in 1946, Stalin is reputed to have responded, 'But what fool will sell us his secrets?'

Berinsfield was founded in 1957, the first new village in England for 200 years. It was on the site of RAF Mount Farm, originally a satellite of RAF Benson, and later a base for the United States Army Air Force. Glenn Miller performed here for American troops shortly before hopping over to RAF Twinwood, and from there to his tryst with death, famously lifting off in a small aircraft on his way to the troops in Paris in December 1944, never to be seen again.

Bullingdon Rural District Council (abolished in 1974) was in charge of the development of the new village, and they named it after local saint Berin, adding the 'field' bit to reflect the fact that it had been an American airfield. The first residents had to make do with the old air base huts, until the new buildings were ready in 1960.

Peacetime is not without its casualties. Little Baldon near Oxford was the scene of an air disaster on 6 July 1965, when a No. 36 Squadron RAF transport aircraft took off from Abingdon en route to RAF Benson and crashed into a field near Little Baldon. Forty-one people onboard were killed, and the tall crops made searching for bodies difficult. An inquest implicated metal fatigue in some of the aircraft's bolts.

There is a commemorative plaque in the church of St Lawrence at Toot Baldon, and a service of remembrance is held every July.

Brize Norton may well have a venerable history stretching back to the Saxons, but today it says just one thing to most people: the RAF, based here since 1937. Indeed, RAF Brize Norton is the largest station in the Royal Air Force, employing 4,500 people. The station has been busy over the last couple of decades, as it is the main airport used for deploying UK troops worldwide. In the current century the military operations in Iraq, Afghanistan and elsewhere have required its services far more often than anyone would like.

In 2012, after the restructuring known as Programme Future Brize, the station welcomed the entire RAF Hercules force, along with new Atlas and Voyager craft. This resulted from a fundamental restructuring of the RAF, and the closure of RAF Lyneham. At that point Brize Norton became the sole station for the embarkation of British troops. Its fleet of craft has risen from thirty to seventy as a result.

In 1946 Harwell Laboratory, the HQ of the Atomic Energy Research Establishment, was opened. Europe's first ever nuclear reactor was built there in 1946, one of five that have occupied the site. The nuclear reactors have now been shut down.

Harwell Laboratory's most infamous occupant was Klaus Fuchs, a German communist who had fled from the Nazis. In 1946 he was made first head of the Theoretical Physics Division at Harwell, but soon fell under suspicion. A joint British and US intelligence operation called the Venona Project had cracked a code through which agents like Fuchs had been communicating nuclear secrets to the Soviets.

In January 1950 Fuchs confessed to MI5 that he was indeed a spy, and was sentenced to fifteen years in prison. The Soviets, allies at this point in history, denied that Fuchs was working for them. He was released from Wakefield Prison after nine years, and lived and worked in communist East Germany until his death in 1988. Upon retirement in 1979 he was awarded the Fatherland's Order of Merit and the Order of Karl Marx.

In the 1940s a member of the Home Guard in Faringdon mixed some Molotov cocktails, to be used in the event of the Germans reaching the town. He then buried the cache in his cottage, on land now covered by the Community College (formerly Tollington School), and promptly forgot all about it.

In 1974 the cache was discovered, and one of the bottles smashed, its phosphorous instantly catching fire. A bomb disposal team from Hounslow defused the DIY bombs, and the war was finally over.

THE OTHER 'OTHER PLACE'

Oxford Brookes University is an amalgamation of colleges and institutions that seems to have been infected by the higgledy-piggledy origins of neighbouring Oxford University. It began life as the Oxford College of Art on the ground floor of the Taylor Institution on St Giles, joined in 1891 by a School of Science with which it merged, in 1934, to become the uncatchily named

'Oxford City Technical School, incorporating the School of Art', with John Henry Brookes (1891–1975) as vice principal. It was now spread over nineteen buildings throughout Oxford, was renamed 'Oxford College of Technology', and moved into much needed new buildings at Headington in the 1950s and '60s.

The institution became Oxford Polytechnic in 1970 and is currently sprawled over various bases, from Wheatley in the east to the former Westminster College at Harcourt Hill in the west, with Headington, Headington Hill and Marston Road in the middle. Since 1992 it has borne the Oxford Brookes name, after its first vice principal.

Clementine Ogilvy Spencer-Churchill, wife of Winston Churchill, was the titular inspiration for Lady Spencer College of Education, built at Holton in 1966. It merged with Oxford Polytechnic in 1974, and now forms the heart of Brookes' Wheatley campus.

Drastic rebuilding took place at the Headington site off London Road and Gipsy Lane in the 2010s, all taken at a bit of a dash following the usual wrestling matches with the local council and residents. At one point demolition was taking place before the final go-ahead for the new build had been given.

A blue plaque to John Henry Brookes was unveiled at his former home at 195 The Slade, Headington, in 2011.

HEADINGTON'S SHARKNADO

A 7m fibreglass Great White Shark called *Untitled 1986* juts from the roof of a Victorian house in New High Street, Headington. It was installed by Radio Oxford DJ and former Balliol law student Bill Heine in 1986, unveiled on the 41st anniversary of the dropping of the atomic bomb on Nagasaki. It was created by sculptor John Buckley, and has survived city council attempts to get it condemned. The shark has become the unofficial emblem of Headington.

The Headington Shark.

Bill Heine's other contribution to the skyline was a set of giant hands and can-can legs installed on the roof of Headington's 'Not the Moulin Rouge' cinema in 1980. The cinema closed in 1991, and the legs were marched off to another cinema owned by Heine in Brighton. Ironically, a planning officer who had opposed the legs when they first kicked off in Headington was now a planning officer in Brighton, out on a limb once again.

BRAVE NEW OLDE WORLDE

Oxfordshire's union workhouses closed their doors in 1929. The last of the county's slums, including St Ebbes' in Oxford, were cleared in the 1950s, and modern housing estates sprang up like ugly poppies amidst the ruins.

In 1974 Oxfordshire devoured a huge chunk of Berkshire, gaining well over 100 settlements. These Johnny-come-latelys include Abingdon, Didcot, Faringdon, Wallingford, Wantage, Wytham, and Oxford suburbs Botley, South Hinksey and Harcourt Hill.

These were not the first to be subsumed or spat out by the fickle county. Mollington has managed to be in three counties. It was originally part of Oxfordshire, Northamptonshire and Warwickshire. A few hundred years ago it lost the Northants bit, and in 1895 the remaining Warwicks' part got swallowed by Oxfordshire.

Village transmigration also occurred in 1844 with the Counties (Detached Parts) Act shuffling settlements between Oxfordshire and its neighbours Berkshire, Buckinghamshire, Gloucestershire and Warwickshire. One Oxfordshire gain was Widford, which had been an isolated chunk of Gloucestershire surrounded on all sides by its new home county. Subsequent nineteenth-century Local Government Acts continued the shuffling, and the last shifts were in 1991 when unpopulated bits on the Bucks/Berks/Oxon borders quietly swapped sides.

In 1968, the various city and county police forces were amalgamated with those of Berkshire, Buckinghamshire and Reading to form the Thames Valley Police Force, headquartered in Oxford. The force is best known for its two most famous sons – the fictional inspectors Morse and Lewis, created by Oxford author Colin Dexter, who later allowed ITV to take up the baton and run with spin-off series *Lewis* and *Endeavour*, all doing their bit to add new angles to the timeless mythology of Oxford and its environs.

Compulsory daily worship was abandoned by the university early in the century; the requirement to have a working knowledge of Ancient Greek was removed in 1920; and in 1960 it was decided that Latin, the linguistic foundation of the Western academic world, was no longer a prerequisite.

For all its outwardly antique air and time-capsule colleges and cobbles, Oxford and its surrounding county had the highest growth rate of 'high-tech' information technology and science-based businesses in the UK during the early twentieth century, the bulk of them tracing their roots back to the university. The trend continues today: Oxford Science Park plays host to around seventy digitally enhanced companies, a fair indication of the thoroughly modern stuff that rushed in to fill the void left by daily worship, Ancient Greek and Latin.

And, to bring this brief Oxfordshire story back to its starting point, in 1972 the Oxfordshire sections of those prehistoric thoroughfares the Ridgeway and the Icknield Way became part of the 140 km-long Ridgeway long distance footpath, running from Avebury in Wiltshire, to Ivinghoe Beacon in Buckinghamshire. With or without its official National Trail designation, this is a route people have been following for more than 10,000 years.

The recurring themes of this book show how history most assuredly repeats itself. Unfortunately, this means that the next bouts of protest and war are a matter of 'when' rather than 'if'. But it also means that the Oxford-based artistic and scientific genius that has fuelled the last 800 years will continue, and that Oxfordshire towns and villages will carry on reshaping and reinventing themselves, and surprising us all in the process. Usually in a good way.

BIBLIOGRAPHY

BOOKS

Boase, Charles William, *Oxford* (London, 1887)

Bompas, George C., *Life of Frank Buckland* (London, 1886)

Brabant, Frederick Gaspard, *Oxfordshire* (London, 1919)

Clark, Sir George, *Oxford and the Civil War* (Oxford, 1970)

Cox, George Valentine, *Recollections of Oxford* (1868)

Davenport, John Marriott, *Oxfordshire Annals* (Oxford, 1869)

Davenport, John Marriott *Oxford, in reference to Laws and Lawyers*, (paper, Incorporated Law Society, Oxford, 1876)

Davies, K.C. and Hull, J. *The Zoological Collections of the Oxford University Museum* (Oxford, 1976)

Ditchfield, P.H. (ed.), *Memorials of Old Oxfordshire* (London, 1903)

Evans, Herbert A., *Highways and Byways in Oxford and the Cotswolds* (London, 1908)

Falkner, John Meade *A History of Oxfordshire* (London, 1899)

Foxe, John, *The Book of Martyrs* (Foxe's Book of Martyrs) (London 1563)

Freeborn, M.E., *'Twixt Cherwell and Glyme* (London, 1900)

Garmondsway, G.N. (ed.) *The Anglo-Saxon Chronicle* (London, 1975)

Garrod, H.W., *The Profession of Poetry and Other Lectures* (Oxford, 1919)

Green, John Richard, *Oxford Studies* (London, 1901)

Hogg, Thomas Jefferson, *Shelley at Oxford* (London 1904)

House, J., *Geography of Oxfordshire* (London, 1870)

How, Frederick Douglas, *Oxford* (London, 1910)

Ingram, James, *Memorials of Oxford*, three volumes (Oxford, 1837)

Jeaffreson, John Cordy, *Annals of Oxford*, two volumes (London, 1871)

Jessup, Mary, *A History of Oxfordshire* (Chichester, 1975)

Lang, Andrew, *Oxford* (London, 1922)

Morris, Jan, *The Oxford Book of Oxford* (Oxford, 1978)

Morris, Jan, *Oxford* (Oxford, 1978)

Murray, John (ed.), *A Handbook for Travellers in Berks, Bucks, and Oxfordshire: Including a Particular Description of the University and City of Oxford and the Descent of the Thames to Maidenhead and Windsor* (London, 1860).

Ovenell, R.F., *The Ashmolean Museum, 1683–1894* (Oxford, 1986)

Parker, James, *Early History of Oxford, 727–1100, preceded by a sketch of the mythical origin of the city and university* (London, 1885)

Peel, Robert and Minchin, H.C., *Oxford* (London, 1905)

Pevsner, Nikolaus and Sherwood, Jennifer, *The Buildings of England: Oxfordshire* (London, 1974)

Plot, Robert, *The Natural History of Oxfordshire* (Oxford, 1677)

Quiller-Couch, Lilian M., *Reminiscences of Oxford by Oxford Men* (Oxford, 1892)

Rapin, Paul de, *The History of England, Volume I*, translated by Nicolas Tindal (London, 1732)

Roberson, George and Green, John Richard, *Oxford During the Last Century: being two series of papers published in the Oxford Chronicle & Berks & Bucks Gazette During the Year 1859* (Oxford, 1859)

Skelton, Joseph, *Oxonia antiqua restaurata* (Oxford, 1823)

Smith, Goldwin, *Oxford and Her Colleges* (London, 1895)

Spiers, R.A.H., *Round About 'The Mitre' at Oxford* (Episodes of the University, City and Hotel) (Oxford, 1929)

Sullivan, Paul, *Bloody British History: Oxford* (Stroud, 2012)

Sullivan, Paul, *The Little Book of Oxfordshire* (Stroud, 2012)

Sullivan, Paul, *The Secret History of Oxford* (Stroud, 2014)

Tames, Richard, *A Traveller's History of Oxford* (London, 2002)

Thorpe, Lewis, *Geoffrey of Monmouth: The History of the Kings of Britain* (London 1977)

Tuckwell, William, *Reminiscences of Oxford* (London, 1901)

Various, *A Handbook for Travellers in Berks, Bucks, and Oxfordshire* (London, 1860)

Various, *History, Gazeteer and Directory of the County of Oxford* (Peterborough, 1852)

Various, *The Zoological Collections of the Oxford University Museum…* (Oxford, 1976)

Walker, John, *Oxoniana: or Anecdotes Relative to the University and City of Oxford* (Oxford, 1806)

Warton, Thomas, *Specimen of a History of Oxfordshire* (London, 1783)

Wells, Joseph, *The Charm of Oxford* (London, 1921)

Wells, Joseph, *Oxford and Oxford Life* (London, 1899)

Whittock, Nathaniel, *Description of the University and City of Oxford …* (London, 1828)

Wood, Anthony, *Athenæ Oxoniensis* (Oxford, 1848)

Wood, Anthony and Hearne, Thomas, *The Life of Anthony à Wood from the year 1632 to 1672* (Oxford, 1772)

Wood, Anthony, ed. Andrew Clark, *Survey of the Antiquities of the City of Oxford, composed in 1661–6, by Anthony Wood,* ed. Andrew Clark, three volumes (Oxford, 1889)

Wood, Anthony, *The Life and Times of Anthony Wood*, abridged from Andrew Clark's edition and with an introduction by Llewelyn Powys (Oxford, 1975)

Young, Arthur, *A Six Weeks Tour Through the Southern Counties of England and Wales*, 2nd edition (Dublin, 1771)

NEWSPAPERS AND JOURNALS

Extant

Banbury Guardian (Banbury)
Daily Telegraph (London)
Folklore (London)
History Today (London)
Oxford Today (Oxford)
Oxfordshire Limited Edition (Oxford)
Past & Present (Oxford)
Social History (Lancaster)
The Times (London)

Discontinued

Bradford Observer (Bradford)
The Burlington Magazine for Connoisseurs (London)
Jackson's Oxford Journal (Oxford)
The Magazine of Natural History (London)
The Morning Post (London)
Notes & Queries (Oxford)
Public Ledger or The Daily Register of Commerce and Intelligence (London)

WEBSITES

www.archeox.net
www.ashmolean.org
www.banburyshireinfo.co.uk
www.bbc.co.uk/oxford
www.berkshirehistory.com
www.british-history.ac.uk
en.wikipedia.org
www.faringdon.org
www.headington.org.uk
www.inoxfordmag.co.uk
www.nationaltrust.org.uk
www.naturalengland.org.uk
news.bbc.co.uk/1/hi/england/Oxfordshire
www.oum.ox.ac.uk
www.ox.ac.uk/colleges
www.oxfordcityguide.com
www.oxford.gov.uk
www.oxfordhistory.org.uk
www.oxfordshirecotswolds.org
oxfordshirelocalhistory.modhist.ox.ac.uk
www.oxfordshire.gov.uk
www.oxfordtimes.co.uk
oxoniensia.org
oxstreets.oxfordcivicsoc.org.uk
www.shotover.clara.net
www.wychwoodproject.org
www.wychwood.co.uk

INDEX